"MYSTERIOUS SCOTT"

The Monte Cristo of Death Valley

AND

TRACKS OF A TENDERFOOT

BY ORIN S. MERRILL

A Story of Modern Mystery of Western Life and the Real Experiences of a Real Tenderfoot, including a Mid-Summer Trip through Death Valley

ISBN 0-912494-10-7
Library of Congress Card Number 72-93067

Printed and Distributed by Chalfant Press, Inc.
Bishop, California 93514
for
Sierra Media, Inc., Bishop, California

PUBLISHED IN 1906 BY

ORIN S. MERRILL, PUBLISHER
CHICAGO, ILL.

COPYRIGHT, 1906
BY ORIN S. MERRILL
(ALL RIGHTS RESERVED)

921
SCOTT

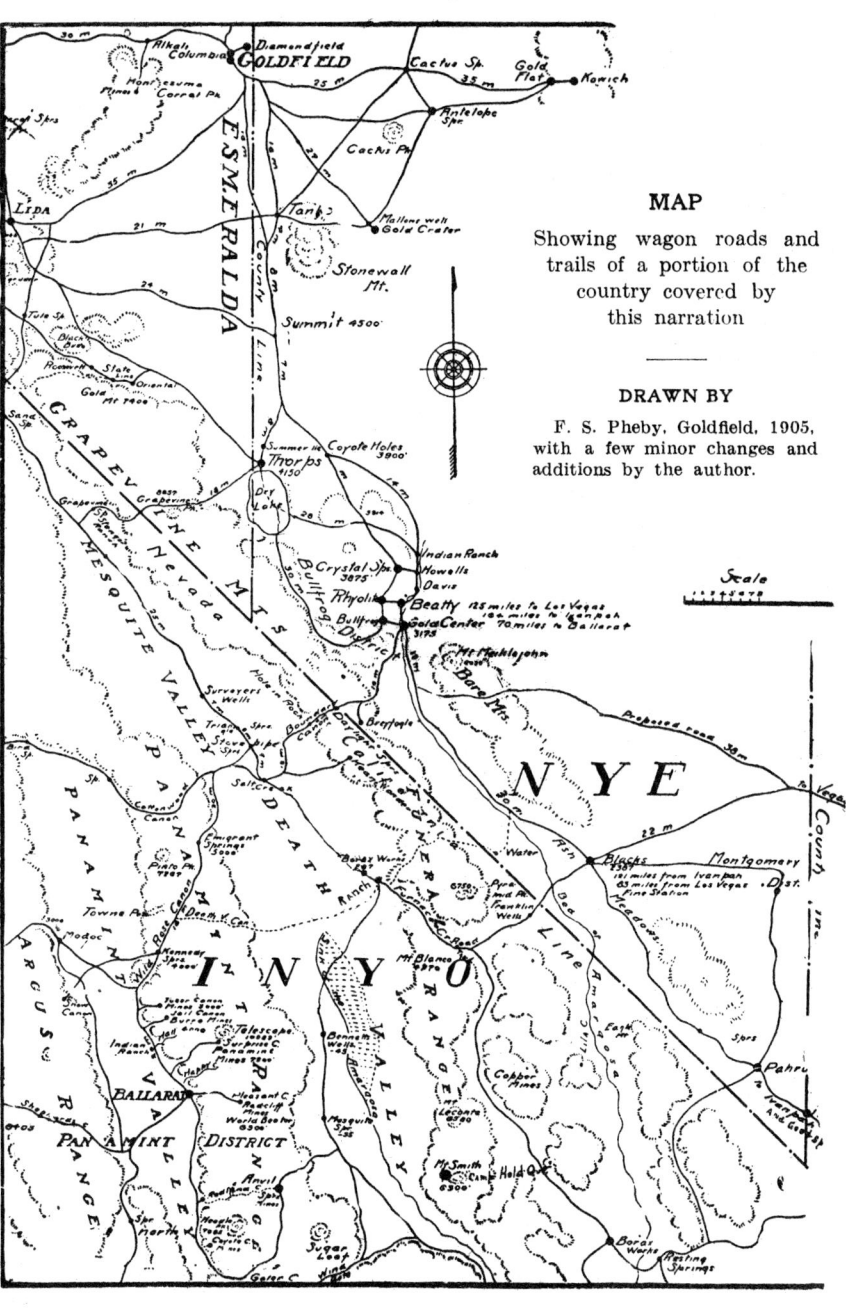

CONTENTS

FIRST DAY IN NEVADA	7
RENO	14
THE BURRO MAN	17
A CHANCE ACQUAINTANCE	21
A NIGHT IN TONOPAH	22
A CITY OF TENTS	28
THE TENDERFOOT BECOMES A MINER	32
GOLDFIELD BY DAY AND NIGHT	33
FOOD FOR THOUGHT	37
STONEWALL SPRINGS—STONEWALL MOUNTAINS	39
SOUTHWARD BOUND	43
A RAINY DAY	47
A NEWLY BORN CITY	49
A "HIKE" BACK TO GOLDFIELD	50
A SEARCHING PARTY AVERTED	52
TWO OPPOSING ARMIES	56
ASH MEADOWS	59
INDIAN CREEK	60
A STRAIGHT TALK	64
NOTHING IN SHORT CUTS	66
AT THE MERCY OF THE DESERT	70
PRINCIPAL DAILY EVENT—STAGE ARRIVAL	75
A CHARACTER	78
AN AFTERNOON AT HOME	79
MILES' AND BROWN'S STORIES	82
RHYOLITE'S FIRST "FOURTH"	87
A TENDERFOOT'S DISAPPOINTMENTS	90
"SCOTTY, THE SCOOTER'S," TRIP	95
DOVES	98
RATTLESNAKE STORY	98
TOWNS OF THE BULLFROG DISTRICT	100
BIRD'S-EYE VIEW FROM FAIR VIEW PEAK	102
HORRORS OF DEATH VALLEY	103
MID-SUMMER VISIT TO DEATH VALLEY	110

Contents

MEN OF THE MOUNTAIN AND THE PLAINS	112
DEATH VALLEY	116
AN OASIS IN DEATH VALLEY	120
THROUGH THE LARGEST BORAX MINE	121
THE PIUTES IN SESSION—GRAND POW WOW	122
SCOTTY'S "CAMP HOLD OUT" FOUND	124
APACHE INDIAN AND DEATH VALLEY MINER	127
A TRIBUTE TO THE BURRO	130
A SUNSET	131
AN AFTERNOON SHOWER	131
LIFE IN THE MOUNTAINS	132
A WORD TO PROSPECTORS	132
"CHUCKAWALLA MIKE'S" STORIES	134
SCOTTY'S PROBABLE DEATH	137
$1,000 REWARD	141
SCOTTY NOT IN "CAMP HOLD OUT"	144
TWO DESERT BATTLES	146
SCOTTY RELATES STORY	148
CORK SCREW CANYON	154

APPENDIX

SPECIAL NOTICE	159
OPPORTUNITIES	161
RECLAIMING THE DESERT	164
SOME MORE RECENT STRIKES	168
MINING REVIEW	169
ADVERTISEMENTS	211

MYSTERIOUS SCOTT
The Monte Cristo of Death Valley

FIRST DAY IN NEVADA

We had left the great Salt Lake early the previous morning, and had been traveling all day through the northern part of the state on the Southern Pacific. We passed through one prairie fire leaping high into the air, that was licking up the grass of the valley for miles and miles. Otherwise nothing of exceptional importance occurred, nothing but what would be liable to happen on any train in any place. The day had taken us through a deserted country; nothing but a barren waste of sand. In the afternoon, we did get into this narrow valley of grass at the head of which we witnessed the prairie fire.

Did you ever travel through a country so unattractive that for want of something to divert your attention, or for amusement, you would for miles and miles count the number of telegraph poles between each mile-post, or take out your watch and "keep cases" on the number of miles you were traveling in so many minutes and together with the aid of your time-table you would figure out how long, at your present rate of speed, it would take you to get to your destination? If so, if you have done these things, then maybe the reader of this book can appreciate how devoid of interest to the ordinary traveler the north-east part of Nevada presents itself. But, as he travels on through the state and gets into these valleys and beholds the beginnings of the hills, the country commences to present to his eye a more pleasant view and to his mind healthier and brighter thoughts.

I was an Easterner, and had first heard of Nevada's wonderful gold fields while on a business trip to Pueblo, Colorado, during the winter months. It was on the tip of every one's tongue there, that a great number of Coloradoans had struck it rich in the New Eldorado, and were right in line to amass large fortunes. While I was pretty well tied financially, having but a "mere shoe-string" for working capital, I had determined before leaving the state to return to my eastern home, wind up some small matters there, and again turn my face westward and give Nevada a whirl. Upon my return home I met a prominent citizen of an adjoining city who had been to Nevada two or three times. He had nothing but good news to give of its prospects of its future. He told how money was so plentiful, that there was more stacked up in the gambling houses there, than was in the banks in his home city; about incidents where those who had struck it rich, had taken handfuls of twenty-dollar gold pieces, and strewn them over the bar-room floor. I also met another business man, of the same city, who had been through Nevada and the Death Valley country some years before who declared that if it wasn't for the education of his children, that would be the place to hold him. He, in turn, told how he had been in locations in that country where the rocks, which were as thick as the cobble stones under our feet (on which kind of pavement we were then standing) could all be panned and every one of them show free gold.

After hearing these glowing accounts which I will have to confess, "went through one ear and out of the other," as the saying goes although I have no doubt that both narrators were adhering to the truth, I found myself on April-fool's day 1905 spending my first evening in Nevada. But, I had lived on the earth too long and had been in business too many years to know that I would find it all peaches and cream. However, I was here to investigate for myself and do for myself.

As we were not due in Reno until midnight, I thought

I would retire and have a few hours rest before our arrival there, where we would have to stay all night as the first train to the new gold fields would not leave until the following morning. With this in view I told the porter to call me one-half hour before we arrived at our destination for the day which he very politely said he would do.

I did not sleep very long, in fact, not long enough, when I awoke suddenly. I looked at my watch and, to my surprise, we were due at Reno some twenty minutes before. Had we made that station and were we beyond it and speeding towards the California line as fast as the train would take us? As we were traveling on time when I retired it looked very much as if such were the case. Well, California might be all right but that wasn't where I was bound for. No place but the new gold fields of Nevada would suit me for the present. I intended to visit California sometime, but not until I had made a stake in Nevada. I remembered that my ticket was good through to Los Angeles if I so desired. Did the porter know this, had he forgotten my instructions the evening before, and was letting me sleep the night through as far as he was concerned? It was evident that such was the case. It was also evident that I was pretty well provoked when that "Honorable" personage appeared upon the scene. I asked him if we were on time. "Yes sah!" I said; "Well, we have left Reno then?" "No sah!" "Well, we are right upon the town then. By my watch we were due there one-half hour ago and I thought I told you to call me one-half hour before our arrival." He replied, "O chile! yo' time is a hull hour off—don't worry. When yo' tell me to does a thing—I does it." I remembered then that there had been a change of time during the night— from Mountain to Pacific time. I know also that upon recalling it—it put me in a more pacific frame of mind.

My reader, if you should ever make this trip allow me to give you a few pointers. Here you want to change your mode of dress if you wish to be one of the people.

You are going into an entirely new field. You can keep on your usual attire but unless you are an outside capitalist and only expect to stay a few days or a week—it is better to change as you will otherwise show too plainly that you are a tenderfoot. Your soft felt hat will do but instead of your stiff bosom shirt and stand-up collar you want a negligee shirt, with a soft lay-down collar, or no collar, no cuffs but those which may already be attached to your shirt If you have been wearing silk stockings change them for 10c per pair socks fairly good weight. You will find they will last as long and give you as good service with boots. If you brought with you three or four pairs of old trousers, worn out at the bottom of the legs, you are in luck, or to be more universally in style a pair of yellow Khaki pants is the thing. (Khaki pants will cost $1.50 per pair; or coat and pants, $3.00). It is even money that your banker will be wearing that make. Don a pair of tan, high-topped, laced boots having the tongue attached all the way up so as to keep out dust and sand. I presume they are the first pair of boots you have worn since those brass-tipped ones with red or green tops, you wore when but a mere lad. You will find out boots are just the thing, easy to get around in and cleaner. Get them fairly good size and do not climb around the mountains much before having them pegged with Hungarian nails on the bottom, which process has a two-fold purpose, to protect soles and heels and to make one more surefooted. Tuck your pant legs inside your boot tops. You need no suspenders nor belt, nor your vest except to carry needful articles such as your watch, compass, etc. You need not worry about being put out of any of the eating houses even if you do not wear a coat.

Well, we are at Reno. If you are attired, as per instructions, you can put foot on Nevada soil with propriety. You might feel somewhat awkward and loose with boots, no suspenders, no belt, and vest unbuttoned, but it is only a matter of time before you will get accustomed to it, and will not feel at home if dressed otherwise. They can still tell you are a tenderfoot by several things. Your boots are shiny and new and probably your clothes are new also. If you have an old pair of pants, they have a neat patch in them, neater than you are liable to get in a mining camp, or you are still clinging to your stiff bosom shirt, white collar or cuffs. There is something to give you away. But, you are doing the best you can, and there are so many tenderfoots coming to this state that you will not be the only one.

Only a Matter of Time.

Of course, when I refer to my readers dressing this way, I am presuming that the reader is of the sterner sex, if I am mistaken, if my reader should be one of the fairer and nobler sex, I have said many things which do not refer to her, and I wish she would take it for what it is worth—diagnose your own case and pick out your own attire, as I am not authority on how woman should dress here or elsewhere. I will say, however, that a felt hat or a cap might be the caper, or if it is during the summer months, a wide-rimmed, high-peaked sombrero is better; fairly heavy shoes is a good thing; no white collars or cuffs; a dress of some good serviceable material, but cool for the summer months. The winter months are mild, but evenings cool. If you enjoy horse-back riding, or if you think you would enjoy it, more than probably you will have an opportunity here, as one does in almost any new community, and of course it is all astride in this country, in which event a divided skirt would not come in amiss among your wardrobe.

I have given you these pointers the best I could, however, do not let the matter of your dress, how to do up your hair, or even your looks, interfere with your coming to this state. I have often thought if I were a young lady—possibly not so young either—just old enough so that I would not care about telling my age any more than I had to—then only under protest—and if I had that home loving temperament, which is characteristic of woman, and my chances were none too promising that I would hie myself away to some new country where the ratio was a 20 to 1 shot. I would there get a position teaching school, or something, and eventually win for myself a home. There is many a worse chap in the city, than the cow-boy of the plains or the young farmer who is pioneering a new agricultural section. The cow-boy more than probably would be a whole-souled, well-met fellow—one who would stay with you to the end. Possibly he has a herd of his own started, or if he has not been of a saving disposition, probably just a word from the right sort of girl—one whom he feels would take an interest in him—and that he knew it wasn't bar-room talk—might be enough to cause him to save his little earnings. The young farmer more than probably would be a progressive, hard-working, companion-wanting individual, tilling his own quarter section of land, thus getting a foot-hold before the country becomes too thickly settled. He might not have his land all paid for, but he has a good starter. The mere fact that these fellows get out of the well-beaten paths into a new country, where they have to strive for themselves without pull or prestige, shows that they have back-bone—a quality that should receive consideration. I know, here in the state of Nevada, of many young men who have made fortunes, and many others are in line to make fortunes; again others are getting better wages than they ever dreamed of at home, or are holding positions of trust in banks or for large mercantile houses; then too there are those who are building up small mercantile businesses of their own, or are getting in on the ground floor of the big things of the country such as mines, town sites, water supplies, local municipal franchises and monopolies. There are also professional men who are building up large practices. A great many of the young business men here are the sons of wealthy sires who have given them a start in a new country in order to get them away from city life. If these men were captured by girls in their home city, it would be considered a lucky strike. Of course, money does not enter into some girls' minds, but to have a fair share of earthly goods, or to have ability to get them has more or less effect on most girls. So, young lady, or older one, if you wish to win yourself a home do not be discouraged but take an old bachelor's advice, and do some pioneering yourself. You will meet with many discomforts, but remember the old adage "All the world loves a lover," and these same discomforts will transform themselves into little features only to be laughed at, and "Laugh and the world laughs with you." These incidents will supply your book of life with memories, that, in after years will be but pleasant pages to look back upon.

If you have to come alone, and make your own livelihood, and you wish to get the best out of life, you must be strong and courageous, but these are a few of the lines you can follow; dressmaking and patching, millinery, teaching, stenography, clerking, running boarding and rooming houses and many other pursuits.

Of course, for those who are not particular as to their

vocation in life there are the dance halls, theaters with bars, saloons, red-light district, and all such galore, but as elsewhere, it is a hard way in the endeavor to seek an easy living.

Now I do not wish to be misunderstood—if your prospects for the future are favorable, or if you have home ties or other good influences that you are taking advantage of, and that you cannot get elsewhere, then do not undertake any pioneering—let the other fellow do the pioneering and come back after you.

Well, I guess I have been "rambling some." When I started out from camp I did not expect to get away so far and stay over Sunday and preach a sermon or two. I must get back to provisions and water. Let me see, it was Reno, was it not, where I branched off, and the time was midnight? I wonder if that last Scotch High-Ball got me in that sympathetic mood?

RENO

We found Reno a "wide-open" prosperous looking town. I was surprised to find a city in Nevada looking so thriving and city-like—wide and well kept streets, and many good business blocks. Regardless of the extremely late hour, besides the drinking resorts, many of the other places of business were open and seemed to be enjoying a good patronage. The city was all lit up. While it was "wide-open" the gambling, nevertheless, was regulated to the second story.

After getting a lunch we endeavored to secure lodging accommodations for the night, which we found to be no easy job and finally, after trying half-a-dozen of the more central hotels and rooming houses, only to get the reply "All full," we were successful in securing a room in a large building across the railroad tracks from the business center; an old orphanage or something that had recently been fitted up for a hotel.

The next morning, after eating our breakfast, we went over to the depot. While our train for the south had the reputation of being one to two or more hours late, as a rule, we found it almost ready to go out on time on this occasion. There was a large, motley crowd assembled awaiting the departure of the train. They all looked as though they belonged to the Mining world in one capacity or another. There were very few women in the crowd. Pieces of baggage were stacked high, one upon another, and the greater share of the passengers could be seen lugging more or less of their essential baggage, such as blankets, etc., instead of having them checked, so as to be sure to have them at their destination. We learned that freight had been so congested there that it was stacked up for blocks around the freight house, and orders had been sent out to railroads not to accept any freight from Reno down, excepting provisions and other necessities of life;—the order stood for several weeks.

As the train pulled out of the depot it was so crowded that many of the passengers had to stand up in the aisles. They were all bound for the new gold fields, and as Goldfield was the center of attraction at that time, and had made for itself a marvelous record, it was catching practically all of them. Every one was talking, and it wasn't long before the stranger had struck up an acquaintance with several of them whom he had been rubbing elbows with, and was feeling right at home. Many of them had been to the camp before—some were already located there, and had been out on a hurried business trip, while others were new arrivals. Their talk was of mines, freighting, and business in general.

Whenever they would mention deals of $5,000, $10,000, $50,000, $100,000, $150,000, or maybe $1,000,000, it would be in such a general way as though it were an everyday occurrence, and the tenderfoot with practically no money or "merely his little shoe-string" would wonder "where in the game would he get on at." But after he had learned that a great many of them who had struck it rich had nothing—possibly had been "grub staked" or had walked into the camp with his pack on his back, or had gone broke and had to secure work in order to again get a foothold—then the tenderfoot with "merely his little shoestring" would take courage—again pull up his pants, which always felt as though they might fall off, and say to himself "What man has done, another man stands the chance of doing" and feel content over the outlook.

It might not come in amiss here to say that the railroad from Reno down to Tonopah is one of the most abominable stretches of railroad that one can find in the United States. The distance is two hundred and forty-four miles, which for the major part, you pay ten cents a mile. Counting the one at Reno, you make four changes to Tonopah, then you take a stage to Goldfield, a distance of twenty-eight miles. The railroad is owned by three distinct companies—The Virginia and Truckee, Carson and Colorado, and The Tonopah Railroad—part is standard gauged, part narrow; the trains are mixed—passenger and freight together; engines are "dinky" ones and the road bed mountainous and uneven. It should be stated however, that it is all being made standard gauge at this time; it is getting into fewer hands and the Tonopah Railroad is building in to Goldfield. The Tonopah Railroad was built by the owners of the Mizpah Mine of Tonopah, from Sodaville, where it connects with the C. & C., down, a distance of sixty-two miles, for the express purpose of hauling its ore to smelters. It was finished August 22nd of last year, 1904. So you see that Tonopah while it has been a good camp for about five years had no railroad until it built one of its own less than one year ago. It is claimed that the railroad not only paid for itself with its first nine months' business, but had $40,000 to the good besides.

It takes from 8:30 in the morning until midnight to make the run from Reno to Tonopah. The tediousness of

THE MONTE CRISTO OF DEATH VALLEY 17

the trip is minimized by several exciting incidents that happen during the day. Then too, there are surprises that present themselves to one who has never been in the state before; for instance—who would ever think by looking at the map of Nevada, of fertile valleys with green pastures. But such is what you see—real pastures with real Jersey cows feeding in them. It shows what these arid lands of these water thirsty deserts can do if just given plenty of water. You pass through this valley, the Carson Valley, for many miles. You see several springs pour out large volumes of water—some of them hot springs, some cold—down this same valley. In another chapter I will tell you how Uncle Sam is reclaiming Nevada deserts that lie in close proximity to the Truckee and Carson Rivers; reclaiming them, under National Irrigation,—for the people—for the home seekers. As you travel further down the line, there are some good looking mountains on your left—mountains that look as though they might carry values with them. On your right you pass Walker's lake which is thirty miles in length and several miles wide; what the depth is at its deepest point is hard to estimate, as it is claimed in places, that it is unfathomable. It is situated in the Walker Indians' Reservation, and as yet the Government has never allowed the Reservation to be prospected by white men. It is thought by some it will be opened up in the near future for settlement and prospecting.

Besides the scenery being new, and the many incidents that happen to help you pass the time on this trip, very probably you'll find some of your newly made acquaintances interesting—I know I did.

THE BURRO MAN

Among others on the train we met a Mr. B. T. Dyer. Mr. Dyer although still a young man had spent several years in Alaska and from his appearance and conversation

I should infer he had made some money there, but the last winter he spent prospecting in Death Valley. He had been on a business trip to San Francisco for a few days and was at that time returning to the gold fields—Goldfield and the more recent camp to the south, The Bullfrog District, which was commencing to receive its share of attention.

Had he been prospecting and making this more or less hazardous trip in the much-talked-of Death Valley region alone? No, his wife had been with him during the entire trip, sharing the hardships with him and being his helping companion throughout and moreover she enjoyed the outing immensely. She was proficient with rifle and held her own in climbing the mountains. It was on this trip that Dyer met the "Burro Man." As I intend to tell you more about this "Burro Man," who is also known by several other names, among the more common ones being "Death Valley Scott," "Mysterious Scott" and "Scooting Scotty" —it might be well for the reader to remember the character also a little bit of history about him might also be opportune at this time.

According to Scott's own story he had spent his still younger days, and he is yet a very young man, on the frontier as a cow-boy. One time he got off further than usual with the herd and accidentally discovered a very rich gold mine. Not knowing what it was he took a chunk of the yellow stuff with him and showed it to the other cow-punchers—who told him it was gold. He afterwards joined the Wild West (Buffalo Bill's) show as a Champion Rough Rider which position he held for several years. He had almost forgotten the gold mine when one day he found himself dead broke. His thoughts then reverted back to it and he secured aid, it is said from a New York banker— President J. N. Girard of the Chamber of Commerce Bank —to return to his once discovered but almost forgotten treasure. His search proved successful. Since then he has been operating it along as he would need pocket money.

He occasionally goes broke it is true, but only after going the extreme limit upon getting out into civilization, which he does, sometimes staying months at a time and spending his money like a millionaire. Who would not call him "Mysterious Scott"—this man of the mines of Death Valley? He has a mine so fabulously rich that he sacks the stuff which is carried out on burros to Los Angeles, or some other important point along the railroad, always getting enormous returns and yet no one knows outside of himself where that mine is located. They know it is in Death Valley, or in the region of Death Valley, more than probable in the Funeral Range, but this is only presumption as "Scotty" himself is the only one that is known to hold the secret. He plays the limit—if he has been doing it merely with a deuce in the hole—he has at least never been called without producing the goods, but he doesn't give them a peep at his hole card only on being called.

It is known that several have tried to track him but he has managed to elude them all. Some of them say they have received broad hints from him—he is a crack shot—that it would be well for them to remain at a safe distance. How true these reports are I do not know. On the other hand—those that know him in society say if he isn't a good fellow well-met he is nothing. He enjoys companionship instead of evading it, but evidently "Mysterious Scott's" notion of being a good fellow among good fellows, that, and being made an object for human parasites or being tracked to his gold mine are entirely two different things. It might be said—figuratively speaking anyway—that in the one he is with you to the finish and in the other he will finish you if you are with him.

It was upon the return of one of these treasure bearing trips to Los Angeles—which city he has been making periodically for the last few years, and the newspapers there had devoted columns to his lavish expenditures of money—that he, with one bunch of his burros, wound up at

Dyer's Camp in Death Valley. As he was there for several days Dyer was able to get quite a bit of his past history from his own mouth which was practically as the above. Dyer said he looked to be a man not over twenty-eight years of age, possibly thirty-one or thirty-two, with a keen eye, pleasing appearance and congenial nature.

Before leaving Dyer told him he did not wish to take advantage of their meeting and their forming an acquaintance, which had become quite mutual, therefore, he would not attempt to follow him. But if he was ready to divulge the location of the mine that he would like to be taken into the game so as to have the chance to acquire some good property for himself. He also asked Scott how he had been so successful in keeping the location of the mine a secret and how he had managed to evade the people that surely had attempted to follow him? "Easy enough" was the reply, upon which he showed Dyer a field glass of extra strong power and one of the best makes money could buy. He told Dyer with that he could sight people in the rear, following him, long before they could sight him in front. He also stated that he had several different bunches of burros (eight, I believe) stationed at various places, here and there, over the country and that when he saw he was being followed he would just side-step them by leaving the bunch of burros he had been riding, make a long "hike" over the country on foot, possibly a great number of miles, to where he had another bunch of burros in reserve and would then again proceed upon his journey.

Upon departing from the camp Scott insisted upon leaving a large assortment of canned goods and boxes of cigars, both of which were of the very choicest brands, and also said that maybe he would give the snap away in regard to the location of his mine and that if he did Dyer was in but that he would have to consider it for a week or so and that if in the event he so decided Dyer would receive a letter from him to that effect. Dyer mentioned he was willing to pay well for a good property but it was the same as putting water on a duck's back—it didn't phase him in the least; he still held out for time. As Mr. Dyer had not received his mail for several days, at the time of this conversation on the train, he did not know whether Scott was ready to spring it or not.

A CHANCE ACQUAINTANCE

When we were within about an hour's ride from Tonopah some one announced that the lights could be seen in the city. Upon the spreading of the news there was a general scramble for the up-lifting of windows followed by the popping out of heads as the journey had been a long one and we were all glad to hear the news and see a mining camp. Finally, as I wished to get a better view of the lighted city in the distance, I went to the rear platform. I hadn't been there long before a young lady, I presume she was twenty-eight or thirty years of age, also stepped out. By the paint on her face and her make-up in general one should judge she might be one of the "fairies" belonging to the "half-world." As she had three or four fair sized valises, and had more or less trouble getting them through the doorway, which was narrow, I loaned her my assistance, which naturally led on to a conversation.

I said "It looks as though you evidently intend staying with the country, judging from the amount of baggage you have."

"That is my intention" was her reply.

"Going to Goldfield, I presume?"

"No, to Tonopah. Are you going to Goldfield?"—she asked.

I replied—"I am. That is where most of them are going."

"You cannot get there to-night can you?"

"No, I'll have to stay at Tonopah to-night and take stage out in the morning."

"How far is Goldfield from Tonopah?"

"That is the new mining camp—twenty-eight miles south," I replied, to which I added—"How do you think you'll like the country?"

"Oh, I like any place where my husband is. Do you know him—Mr. So and So?"

To which I replied—"No, I am a stranger here. This is my first trip."

"He promised to meet me at the train. I don't know what I will do if he isn't there. Where do you intend to go for the night?"

"Oh, I don't know. Up-town to one of the hotels I presume."

To which she replied—"Maybe he'll be there though. We'll see." Whereupon the train commenced to slacken up. It had not yet come to a stand-still when a young man swung himself upon the steps of the rear platform. As she could not see him plainly she asked in an emphatic voice—"George, So and So, calling him by name, is that you?" At which he looked around and she again asked—"George, you lovey-dovey, that is you is it not?" To which he replied—"Sure it's me. How are you Floss?" "Oh, fine hubby," whereupon they embraced and had a hug and a kiss. After this salute she said—"I wasn't sure whether that was you or not, but I thought it was. You wrote me you would wear a felt hat and a red neck-tie so I took the chance anyway."

Thus, as the train stopped, they became lost to view—this "man and wife"—whom I do not presume ever saw one another twice before in their life. Did you say—"whole life?" Yes, I mean twice before in their "whole life."

A NIGHT IN TONOPAH

Tonopah you will find a "wide-open" town of one business street. I should judge it is at its zenith at midnight. To go up town you have to go two or three blocks from the depot. You pass the dance hall half way up. They are playing a two-step and at this time the dance is on full swing. If you should give a side glance in as you pass by you will notice the girls are all dressed in decidedly abbreviated costumes—decidedly abbreviated both top and bottom. The men are dressed in all styles. Some can be seen wearing "kicks" and some shoes, but these as a rule are jauntily dressed, and are beardless. The larger number however have on high-topped laced boots or booties, which are rusty with wear, a Khaki or corduroy pair of pants—no suspenders, their shirt is as liable to be unbuttoned at the top as not and they have anywhere from a two weeks' to a two months' beard—some of the beards are clean and well kept, a few are filled with the dirt of the dusty road or are rusty from knocking around the mountains. This latter class—the fellows in boots—are those who have found the wealth of the country—some sold out for a mere song, others managed to retain large holdings. A very few of the dancers wear coats. The men in the boots might be awkward but they need not fear treading on the trail of a partner's dress. I could not understand at first why all the girls wore the abbreviated skirts—which are above their knees—I do now—it is so their dresses will not be stepped upon—they are a good thing.

You go up town and engage your room—it is an alcove curtained off of the hotel office. There are two beds in the room but you can have the single bed for $2.00 per night—its the best they have, everything else is filled up—you're lucky to get that. As I said before, your room is only separated from the office-room by a curtain. The office-room is also used as a bar-room and a sort of a gambling room—two games of chance going, a roulette wheel and a faro game.

As there is too much noise in the office and as the town seems thoroughly awake you decide not to retire right away but instead take a stroll around. Any saloon you might drop into you'll find a goodly number at the bar besides the more private parties. These private parties are at one side in boxes only separated from the rest of the room by a 2 x 4 inch railing—they consist of men and women about two or three men, to one woman. They are drinking champagne and apparently having a glorious time. Many of the champagne drinkers have always been on a beer salary before coming to this camp, but, they have struck it rich and spend their money freely.

If you are "frisky" and wish to go up against the tiger or if you are home-sick, or are thinking too strongly of the girl you left behind that gave you the answer "No" and you have the blues too badly and wish to divert your mind —you might drop into the Tonopah Club. You will find it a large gambling house situated on the ground floor on the principal street of the city. You with the blues if you bought chips and if you are jogging along in your play and your mind is still not diverted and you wish to play them higher—or higher—or still higher—you may do so, in fact, I guess you may play any amount you might wish—it being only limited by your own chips you may have in front of you. If you have a streak of luck and win in your big plays you need not fear but what you will get cash for your chips; if you lose, of course that is a different thing, you lose,—what is, is.

The proprietors of this resort are said by those who are in a position to know, to have made upwards of a good five million dollars in the last few years. They are not only gamblers but are also mining men and besides their present holdings they are always looking for more. They are more liable to have from thirty to forty prospectors in the field at any time, scattered in different parts of the state, whom they are grub staking, than not.

While I am writing about gambling I could tell you of a little play that came up quite recently. The print in the big newspapers of this country telling about it is hardly cold at the time of the writing of this article in which the central figure was a party—a mining man, not only of a national reputation but a world wide reputation—being known across the waters to even a greater extent than here It did not happen in the Tonopah Club, nor did it happen even in the city of Tonopah, but it did happen in the state. The man referred to did not feel "frisky" as he is considered a very conservative mining man—nor is it thought he had the blues—he "just wished to while away a little time." He bought chips and commenced to win from the start. When he cashed in he was $20,000 to the good.

I can tell you of other incidents where they were not so lucky—one in particular of a local party here who had made good money in the state, in the last fifteen months, out of mining. I guess this party felt "frisky" all right—anyway, he managed to drop $28,000 before the night was over. This reminds one of the old saying "Easy comes and easy goes." As he had some good properties, I presume that amount did not represent more than one fiftieth of what his holdings are worth—all of which he made in a year's time starting with "No funds on hand."

These plays do not happen every day but they are of a very common occurrence and I enumerate them only because I consider them pretty fair for the desert. There are "plungers" here as well as in Wall Street.

Well, Tonopah looks good to me, but as I was bound for the more recent gold fields I cannot tarry here long but I will promise my readers to bring them back again if only for a brief stay.

It was in the small hours of the morning when we retired and yet things were still lively. They were also still alive when we rolled out to take our farewell of the burg later on in the same morning. As for myself I know I got very little sleep as they were doing business all night long in that room they used for the combined purpose of office, saloon, baggage room and gambling hall, so if one did not hear the loud talking of the customers at the bar, which was almost continuous and which nearly drowned all other noises, then it was the whirl of the wheel and the rattle of chips.

I said it was still alive in the morning, but the main business of the morning was done by almost an entirely different set and I also noticed that there were not as many women in evidence as there were the night previous.

Besides the general run of business one can see in operation in most any town of its size, those that appealed to my eye by far most of all, as I was not as yet familiar with them, was the army of men busy freighting, and the prospectors, besides the stage drivers and the automobile chauffeurs.

There were several freighting wagons that were finishing loading up, and pulling out. The command of the driver, who sat on one of the rear horses with a single rope in hand to guide a team of twelve to twenty horses or mules, the tingle of the bells of the lead team, the rattle of the chains of the others as they tightened up on their tugs, and finally the muffled rumbling of the wagon, with a trailer or two attached, each heavily loaded, was all new to me. Then there were the prospectors, each packing his bunch of burros preparatory to going to the mountains, while the stage drivers were busily getting their baggage loaded and rounding up their passengers as were also the automobile chauffeurs.

They all presented a busy sight—these transportation companies—transporters of freight and passengers far across the desert—across to a country that has been until very recently overlooked by man.

We had not decided on transportation for ourselves as yet when "Tex," the stage driver, ran across us. It wasn't three minutes until we had engaged passage with him, and he had loaded on our baggage so as to clinch the deal. If it ever will be your lot to come to this western country and you are looking for transportation, and you run across "Tex" and he has transportation to sell—put it down that you are landed right then and there. He has that talk and way about him that sells the goods—he might have been out the night before but he is all business the next day.

As we had upwards of three-quarters of an hour, before the departure of the stage, I availed myself of the opportunity to go around to the dumps of some of the mines which were only a little over a stone's throw from the business center. In my journey I learned the history of the discovery, less than five years before, of the vast wealth there and why they named the first two prospects, which are large producing mines now, the "Mizpah" and the "Tonopah." I would really liked to have stayed there a few days, so as to come in touch with a real mining camp —one that has had the test of time diligently applied to it as to its worth—before going on to the more recent diggings—but, I felt as though this sight-seeing might not be, temporarily, the healthiest thing for my "mere shoe-string."

Thus it was at nine o'clock on said morning—the third of April, I believe, in the year of our Lord 1905, that we found ourselves in a four-horse stage on the way to Goldfield, where I expected to stay for a few days, then push on to the more recent camps of Bullfrog, where I expected to ultimately locate. The rate from Tonopah to Goldfield by stage is $4.00 the person; by automobile, $6.00; fifty pounds of baggage is allowed each person. A few weeks before our arrival there were so many flocking into the country that they had to register at Tonopah one week before hand in order to procure a ride out.

We found "Tex" a very interesting personage. He had lived for a number of years in South America and had also belonged to Buffalo Bill's Show during which time he had toured over all the states, besides England and a great many more of the European countries.

We passed a great number of freight teams, from four to twenty head in a team, bound in the same direction we were. Some had loads of lumber, some tents, some general merchandise of all sorts, while some were loaded with machinery. Other large teams we met, they being bound for Tonopah. These had cargoes of ore—all sacked, and in a couple of cases these cargoes were guarded by men on top armed with Winchesters. At noon we stopped at Ramsey's Wells where we got a very good dinner for fifty cents.

A CITY OF TENTS

We could sight Goldfield several miles off. It looked to me as though it was three or four miles off when in reality it was fifteen. We found the roads quite sandy for a few miles and "Tex" told us at times the wind blew the dust so that one couldn't see the horses in front. On this trip it wasn't so bad—but bad enough.

The country between Tonopah and Goldfield is a plain devoid of grass. The only vegetation is the sage and grease-wood brush, some cactus, and a tree known as the Joshua, dotting the country, singly, here and there. Just before you enter the city, the town of Diamondfield which you pass, can be seen to the left two or three miles, and Columbia Mountain around whose base you go lies in front and to your left. This mountain is quite prominent as it towers above the others and stands alone. You cannot see the town because it is protected by the mountains, but the town of Columbia lies beyond—nestled at the base of that mountain of the same name—and still beyond it lies Goldfield, with a high mesa on the right side and the outcropping of mountains on the other.

Columbia—which by the way grew up in a night—and Jumbo, which is still further to the left, and Goldfield are practically one town, or it might not be out of the way to say city. It is surely a city of tents. It had a half dozen in November, 1903. Now, it has a population of 10,000, the largest city in the state. There must be some reason for this rapid settlement. It is these hills, these out croppings, which can be seen in ridges here and there that is the cause of it all. The topography of the country is not cliffy, but low to be called mountainous—easy of access. These out croppings look to be of a volcanic nature. The general formation is porphyry. The altitude is about 6,000 feet.

Goldfield we found to be a very busy and crowded city. The sidewalks, of plank, and each section of a different elevation than that of the adjoining lot, were thronged with people; as were also the stores, especially can that be said of the drinking places and these were numerous.

Very few of the men looked as though they were down on their luck. You could tell these when you saw them. Instead of their being in and one of the crowd they would be lingering out on the edges. Occasionally you would see an isolated case like that—one that would prick up his ears and make a quick move only when he heard some one tell the bartender to give the house a drink—but they were few.

The crowds that were congregated in groups were composed mainly of those that were off shift, or prospectors that were in for a few days, or representatives of capital, people who would not take a job if it was tendered to them on a silver tray; not in a gold camp like this. There were also those who would like to have been busy. They were the ones who had been leasing. That was when the times had been the flushest, and the money was being taken out of the ground, by a few hundred thousand dollars a month more than was being put into it. The mine owners had recently, on account of the large productiveness of the mines, changed the system from leasing to no leasing and were going hereafter to work the properties themselves. Many of these properties that had hitherto been leased at a big profit to the leaser had not yet had time for the reorganization and another large producer was in litigation, but everything possible was being done in these properties to speed things along and get down in a systematic manner under the new management. New mills were being constructed, new machinery installed. and mains laid for miles to convey water. Up to date little ore had been worked, but what had, ran upwards of $100.00 to the ton as it all had to be freighted for miles over-land, then shipped out over four different railroads to Salt Lake City to be treated. Everything else was high, material and cost of living, on account of the freighting. Ore that ran less than $100.00 per ton would not pay, consequently it would not be mined or would be left on the dumps. There was plenty above that mark though as the leasers—and many of them were poor men before—who had made vast fortunes are numerous.

No one had anything but a good word to say for the camp. The man that didn't even have money in his pockets—had made good wages but gambled it—had nothing but praise. The leasers and prospectors who had not struck it yet were all hopeful and optimistic. They knew what others had done and were glad to have the chance to do the same—their day was liable to come at any time.

I found the people that comprised Goldfield came from all over the world, especially from mining countries. A great number were from Colorado, Utah, and Montana; the Coeur d' Alenes—wherever that is—were mentioned quite often; native sons from California were there and miners from Arizona; then there were the placer miners from Alaska that wanted to try quartz mining in Nevada—and many from England, Australia, Africa, Old Mexico, Hawaii, and I know not where, but they all thought well of the state.

It seemed queer to pay more for the three poles (ridge pole and two end poles) and stakes for a 10 oz., 10 x 12 ft. tent than what the tent cost in your home town, or to pay $2.50, without Hungarian nails, or $3.00 with, for the half-soling of a pair of $3.00 shoes; or to pay as much for a new glass for your compass as it would cost for the entire compass in the east, but such were the conditions. I know I also paid $1.50 to an expressman for his services, no lifting, for fifteen and one-half minutes, by my watch, from the time I engaged him until he was back to the same place he started from and paid off, and he told me that was a reduced rate.

A shave would cost you 25c; neck shave, 10c extra; hair cut, 50c; singe, 50c; face massage, 50c; tub bath, $1.00; shoe shine, 25c. A few of the laundry prices were as follows:—shirts, 25c; shirts with collars and cuffs attached, 30c; undershirts, 20c; collars, 7½c; cuffs, per pair, 15c; socks, 5c; handkerchiefs, 5c; etc.

All drinks were 15c, or two for "two bits," except egg drinks, which were "two bits" a piece. If you wished a glass of beer you would pay 15c for it—no schooner either —very far from it—the same size glass as you would get if you were some places and paid $1.00 for a bottle and treated the house of seven or eight.

You could get your home paper from newsboys, who had carts on the street corners and advertized "Papers from all parts of the World," for 10c per copy for papers in the states. Meals were quite reasonable—a fifty cent piece, or "four bits" as they call it here, would buy one a fair meal; ice to the largest consumers was 5c per pound and water delivered to your tent was $1.00 per barrel. One barber told me that his water bill for the previous month for his shop was $176.00, that included about 300 baths. Many houses were bringing rent of $20.00 per room per month—a six-room abode $120.00 or a one-room box tent house, $20.00, but most people would bring their own tent which they would buy in the east and have it checked through as baggage. One can get a city lot from town site people very reasonably or if you wished to go out a little way one will have no trouble to find room for his tent as it is all government land anyway.

These prices all sound pretty high but by having his own tent and keeping bach, which most of them do, one can live on from $18.00 to $20.00 per month. Of course, that does not include nicknacks but stuff that sticks to the ribs and plenty of it.

Wages for the least-paid man with pick and shovel on streets, was $4.00 per day of eight hours; barbers paid their janitors $5.00 per day; grocery clerks, $5.00 per day; miners, $4.00 per day, but many of the leasers paid considerably more than the scale—seven days in the week—very few knew when Sunday came. Jobbers, with a two-horse team, clear upwards of $600.00 per month; stage drivers with four-horse teams clear of expenses from $500.00 to $1,000 per month and everything else in comparison.

THE TENDERFOOT BECOMES A MINER

I arrived in Goldfield Monday afternoon, commenced work Wednesday morning following. It was on a lease. It was the first time I ever had any real downright labor to do and when noon came around the first day I was pretty tired and my muscles sore. We had an hour and a half nooning though and that helped out considerably. At night I was very tired but felt really better than I did at noon and the second night found me better than the first and by the end of the first week my soft muscles were getting hardened up in fairly good shape—quitting time would come around before I would notice it; instead of looking at my watch every few minutes and thinking it never would come as I had done the first few days. Although the property was out a mile and a half I managed to get down town almost every evening, as the mining world was new to me and I wanted to get in touch with conditions the best I could. As I had met with financial reverses the last few years I felt pretty cautious with my "mere shoe-string" which I had left—in fact, too cautious.

I stayed with the job for about one month during which time I had held almost every position in a mine-to-be; hoisting with a hand windlass, wheeling a wheelbarrow, mucking, picking and drilling. They never allowed me to set off the fuse or I never sorted ore or "high graded." As we never struck any pay ore, as the best assay was $6.53, I could not hold the last two positions. Did you ask what was "high grading?" Well, if you do not know I will not tell you. Your mother taught you that "Honesty is the best policy." You cannot live up to your mother's teachings and "high grade" too.

As it was a lease on which we were working and as it would terminate some day and as the leaser wished an extension in time and a concession or two, he thought it would be good policy to shut down for a time, while he was sparring for time as he knew if he ever ran into the real stuff his requests would not stand much of a chance in being granted, so one day we were given notice that we would close on Saturday night, temporarily at least.

So, when Saturday night came we were without a job, as I was "champing at the bits" to get out prospecting or to make money faster I was not much disappointed.

GOLDFIELD BY DAY AND NIGHT

Goldfield is a hustle and a bustle town, for a small city, during the day as well as at night. There are the automobiles going hither and thither with passengers, some going out, others heavily covered with dust coming in. They are a great thing for the desert and are always going and coming from Lida on the west, Kawich on the east, Tonopah on the north and the towns in the Bullfrog District on the south. These later towns are getting the most of the traffic. Then there are the four-horse stages, while they are not in evidence as often as the automobiles they can carry more passengers at a time, some carry eight or nine and a few as high as twelve and in case of a pinch they are often seen to carry twelve to sixteen passengers each, besides a great amount of baggage. While the stages may not make the speed the automobiles can, their prices are considerably lower and with their increased capacity, as each automobile doesn't carry over five, counting the chauffeur, the stages have the greater amount of the transportation.

Large freighting wagons are unloading or loading their cargo all the time, while smaller ones of two horses instead of eighteen or twenty, are bringing in building stone from near by quarries that have been opened up. This stone is for two or three stone buildings that are being erected at the present time. On account of so many canvass and frame buildings and their heretofore inadequate water facilities, but which are being improved, insurance has been an almost impossible thing to procure.

Ready for the Mountains.

A few burro outfits can be seen. Some are getting provisions to go out, while another has an outfit to sell. Burros are selling from $30.00 to $50.00 a piece and upwards. The number of prospectors from Goldfield would make a fair-sized regiment. When a Goldfieldite says "out from Goldfield" he means there are that many in the state and as they all make Goldfield some time or another and as it is the principal point of attraction this Spring the claim is not without some foundation. This seems quite a number of "knockers" to be out with their little hammers knocking away at the country but as the state is large and the mineral resources great, their knocking is of a beneficial character instead of a detrimental one.

Recently, before they had post-office boxes here, the influx to the city was so great for the corps of postal clerks that a person would have to stand in line, or pay a small boy $1.00 to do it for him, the greater portion of the forenoon in order to get his mail.

Every one in a mercantile business was making money, also brokers, many leasers, property owners and many divers lines. One man, a Hebrew, in the General Merchandise business had started with $500.00 capital and was reputed to have made $75,000 since coming to the camp. A great number could be cited that had made a greater amount than that on less capital but they had struck it in mining—while this party made it in the mercantile business.

Along in the afternoon the crowds commence to congregate in the street and drinking resorts. A great many of the miners commence work early in the morning and "knock off" early in the afternoon, putting in their eight hours; thus along the latter part of the afternoon, it is a large and motley crowd. The man with big money can hardly be told from the man with small means as they are all attired about the same—negligee shirt—Khaki pants—boots etc.

A half-score of the more prominent saloons have a large crowd, although many of those that assemble there are not people one would class as drinking people, but the saloons are about the only places that are "wide-open" to the public—where one man can meet another or where he can get in touch with men in general and new happenings in the camp and also new strikes on the outside. As I said before, there are a half-score of the more prominent ones that are packed as thick as bees in a hive besides those in front on the sidewalk. There would be almost as many people in each one of these saloons as there would be at a funeral in a country village where the most prominent person of the community had died. As each of these large saloons would be a gambling house too—all on the ground floor—there would be games going galore. Each saloon would have as many as five, six, seven or eight games in operation. There would be a crowd lined up and more than probably a couple of ladies —large plumes in hats—lined up with them to the bar—full length and two deep and then some couldn't get lined up, and the bar is not of a short length either. There would also be others playing the games besides those that didn't participate in either.

It would not be an uncommon occurrence to see a lady playing roulette putting quite a stack on this number, quite a stack on that—sprinkling her bets here and there all over the table—taking her losings good-naturedly or her winnings in an exceedingly happy manner but betting her money freely; or to see a woman, some madam, with several large diamonds on her fingers—sitting at the faro table incidentally "keeping cases" but mainly betting her money—but such is the case. While women do not comprise more than one-twentieth of the patronage of these resorts they are at times in evidence good and plenty.

Maybe at another saloon there is a man betting his money pretty stiff; for instance—instead of having white chips he is using twenty-dollar gold pieces. Another is trying to appease his taste. He has acquired an appetite for champagne and a love for women since he has made a lucky strike or two and is letting loose of some of his money by buying drinks for a group of acquaintances.

Then there are the girls at the theaters, we do not want to forget them. One of them will do a stunt—sing a song or dance a few lines or both—after which the curtain will drop and it will stay dropped for a quarter of an hour, but, it is all right you did not have to pay any admission to get in or you will not have to pay any to get out. During this period all the girls will do a stunt by priming you up, or trying to prime you up, to buy a drink and drinking, after which the curtain will again rise—another song or a dance or possibly a one-act play by four or five of them—and so on.

Then there are the girls at the dance halls, which are down the line further. It does not matter if you have on heavy boots or if you do not know how to dance. They are willing to teach you. After each dance you bolt up to the bar with the young lady and have a drink, then another dance and a drink, and so on.

FOOD FOR THOUGHT

If I was a preacher I could preach a sermon on "tainted money" right here. Here is a mining camp; the wealth is being taken out of the ground by the sweat of the brow in the shape of ore. This is sent to the smelters to be treated and put into gold bullion, after which Uncle Sam's stamp is put on it and it is returned, or its equivalent, to the people that have been instrumental in one capacity or another in taking it out—mine owners, leasers, promoters, or laborers, they are the ones who have profited by it directly.

Thus ore which is transformed into money—the medium of exchange through which all earthly goods are bought—is dug out of the earth and returned to the producers. It is through the channels of gambling, wine and women that a great share of the ore, or rather its equivalent money (if not the same dollars then other dollars that represent it) first goes after coming out of mother earth. Is it this newly made money that has not yet been put into use that first goes through these channels that does the mischief in the world, no matter in what channels it might happen to get thereafter? You will say "But there is some money that comes into a camp, for instance, outside money that is put into an unprofitable mine, but that also gets into these channels. What have you to say about that?" That outside money while it did not come from this camp came from some other. They have the same kind of life in that producing camp where that $1.00 of yours came from as here. Life here is no different than in other producing camps.

The farmer gets a crop of potatoes, or a crop of corn, or the manufacturer makes a pair of shoes. They cannot have their potatoes, corn, or shoes made into potato bullion, corn bullion, or leather bullion and then have Uncle Sam's stamp put on to it and henceforth act as a medium of exchange. If so—the same question could be put to potatoes, corn, or a pair of shoes, or anything else that is produced, if it answered for a medium of exchange. But as money covers all as it buys all, I take money as an example.

Is it the money that goes through these channels that causes the mischief in this world? Of course, a great share does not go through these channels but to some elevating use. If we start these dollars off right for the first time will they always act right? If it gets into these channels, which is—we will all have to admit—not attaining the greatest possible amount of good, it has to get out again if it attains that greatest possible amount of good. They say to remedy an evil strike it in the bud. If our mining camps were all pure, would the entire civilized world that uses coin money as a medium of exchange be pure?

Or, to put it in different words—if the money's first use was put to the greatest possible use would it ever be put to a use that wasn't good?

Or to look at it from another side—if a really good person, a benefactor to mankind, should acquire all this money after it had first gone through these channels—got it some way where he gave them "value received" in earthly goods—food, clothing, or say education—would this money ever be the cause of giving this benefactor of mankind any grief?

Or, to look at it still another way—If a girl of the red-light district used this money, which she earned in her pursuits, to educate a virtuous sister (her sister or her sister's instructor need not know where the money came from) would that education be beneficial or detrimental to that virtuous sister?

Does the first use of newly made money, or the first use of any other medium of exchange as far as that goes, change human nature, outside of the effect it has directly and indirectly from that first use?

Can it be used to do the very rankest kind of deed and then its very next use be a noble and inspiring one?

Is a gambler's money as good to build churches on as any other money?

Are there certain dollars in this world that are doing good deeds all the while no matter in whose hands they happen to be and another set of dollars that is making people unhappy all the while no matter in whose hands they may get?

This might be food for thought.

STONEWALL SPRINGS—STONEWALL MOUNTAINS

By getting in touch with different prospectors that would come in, one could get acquainted with the lay of the country and its possibilities in a general way in fairly good shape. They would be from Lida way, Echo Canyon Telescope and Funeral Range, from the Bullfrog District Kawich, and all over, so one would be liable to frequently hear of new strikes in most any direction.

The expressions one would hear in regard to the mineral possibilities of the state, with very few exceptions, if any, were very encouraging to the man with practically no money. He might be poor one day and in a month from that time have a gilt-edged looking prospect. As one miner put it—"It is so good, that if a person tells the truth of Nevada an outsider will think he is crazy." You would often hear remarks similar to this and they would come also from miners that had not as yet struck it—had not made a cent out of the country—had nothing to sell or who were boosters for no one.

At this time there became quite an exodus to the Bullfrog District as there had been several new important strikes made there and it was becoming the center of attraction. Every one was talking Bullfrog. Reports would come back "While Tonopah and Goldfield are not so slow, that Rhyolite, the Bullfrog District was the limit."

A prospector by the name of O'Brien—W. S. O'Brien —had been out south and west of Lida—across the state line into California—and had just returned for a few days and wanted the boys, who had been working in the same mine as myself, and I to go out there prospecting. He said he could put us on to some good looking mountains that should be prospected. He had staked off a few claims and thought they had merit. He was going back in a few days and said he wanted to see us out there. He was so enthused with the country that he got us almost in the same mood.

We had not decided to go to Lida for sure—the other boys got a job that would hold them for a few days and I had been out of work for a couple myself—when I commenced to get restless—restless to go some place and fill in the time—so on the third morning as we were eating our mush, ham, pancakes and coffee, I inquired the distance to some of the different camps. I informed them that I thought I would take a "hike" over and back to that large mountain pointing to the south and east. They told me "it is further than it appears by a h-ll of a sight. You will not be able to make that and back in a day by a long ways."

Before I made up my mind to go for sure and got things in readiness it was 9 o'clock in the morning. I managed to find an old canteen—it had a small crack in it but I thought that would cut no ice. So with a leaking canteen (I filled it with water on the start at any rate) and a ham and egg sandwich in my pocket, my oldest duds on my back, a hammer and a small pan and some money in my pocket I started out on foot. It is needless to say that after I made two or three pannings and took a few swigs of water as it was leaking out anyway, together with the leaking, that I was out of Adam's Ale in less than three hours. But, as I saw snow in the crevices of the mountain I was making for I presumed I could get my thirst quenched somehow and anyway I did not like the idea of going back without getting to my destination. I also got along so far that I knew if I turned back night would overtake me and I would be tied up in the mountains and nine chances out of ten I would get lost. In that event it would be hard to tell when I would get back to Goldfield. I preferred making the mountain—staying in it all night—taking chances in finding a spring or getting to the snow in the morning rather than take chances in turning back.

I had been in high altitudes and mountainous countries long enough to know that distances were deceiving. I had a certain point in that mountain that I was making for. It looked as though there was a spring there and anyway it was about the nearest point to go to. By drawing a beeline with my eye, between that point and myself, I felt I could almost count the grease-wood bushes that lay in my pathway or guess within a small margin how many one-hundred yards it was, but I noticed it took me several hours after that to get to the place. I arrived about five o'clock in the afternoon. There was a nice spring there as I had anticipated. There was quite a flow of water but the stream it formed was like so many streams I have seen in Nevada since—it went a few hundred feet then lost itself all of a sudden in the ground.

The springs had been filed on by two different parties. I noticed by the location papers it was known as the

"Stonewall Springs." The first filing was for mill site purposes, that was dated about two months before and the work done. The last filing was dated as recently as the day previous to my arrival and was for agricultural, grazing and domestic use. The filer couldn't more than have gotten it up until he was notified in rather impressive terms to remove it, as this inscription was on the bottom of his notice in heavy lead pencil—

TAKE THIS NOTICE DOWN. SEE—

I presume the threatener would have used red ink if he had been able to procure it.

I was not the only camper at the springs as there were a couple of prospectors with a four-burro outfit there also. One of them was a French man by the name of Pete, as I learned afterwards, and by the way he has since struck it rich, and his partner. They had unpacked and just finished their supper when I got to the springs.

I still had my egg and ham sandwich. It had been my intention to find some hole in a rock so as to crawl into it, to keep out of the wind, build a bonfire and endeavor to keep as comfortable as possible until the sun came out warm in the morning when I would get a nap as I knew it would be too cool to sleep at night. Then I would make for some place to get a meal, either back to Goldfield or elsewhere.

They noticed I had only a sandwich with me and offered me supper. Nothing would do but that I accept it. They also had extra blankets they were not using, so through their hospitality I had supper—slept under blankets—and breakfasted the next morning. Although I did make them take pay for the breakfast which they did unwillingly. After supper they hobbled two of their burros, so the pack would not stray away too far during the night, and put a bell on the leader, so as to readily locate them when they so desired.

As there were tufts of good grass thickly growing at the base of the mountain and a fine spring of good water it was an ideal place to camp. We also gathered some soft downy brush from which we made our bed and with a canopy of clear sky bedecked with the bright moon and stars over our heads—I for one enjoyed the sleep. It was the first time I had slept out in the open for many a year, but I am not sorry to say it has not been the last.

After breakfast in the morning we went our divers ways, into the highness of the mountain, and spent the balance of the day prospecting. At noon I had my sandwich and plenty of water and at night I wound up at Stonewall Tanks, a station on the route from Goldfield to Bullfrog. "The Tanks" is located about seven miles from the spring but they haul water from the springs there to satisfy man and beast, on their pilgrimage across the desert, for which they charge a nominal sum.

SOUTHWARD BOUND

During the night I made up my mind to keep on going to Rhyolite where I originally intended to go or rather to the Bullfrog District, as Rhyolite was unknown when I was still back east. I said to myself—"I have really stayed in Goldfield working too long now—Why be sidetracked and possibly pass up a good thing? It is a very new camp and every one is speaking well of it. That is where I wanted to get —into the newest good camp going. I will investigate for myself. If I do not like it I can then get back to Goldfield before the boys go to Lida prospecting anyway."

In the morning I wrote three or four letters. One of

them was to one of the boys telling him of my intentions.

I did not have much money in my pocket to travel in this country on but I determined to make the trip anyway. I had money coming for services but as that had to come from the main office it would take some days yet at any rate. I also had my original "mere shoe-string" it is true, but that was in the shape of a New York draft. I, being a stranger, it would be impossible for me to realize on it. Even if I could have realized on it immediately I would have hesitated, before breaking into it to make the trip, as I did not care to cut into it merely for sight-seeing purposes—unless I knew what the future, barring accidents, had in view for me. But anyway it would be impossible for me to get it cashed. I knew no one in Rhyolite and I believed it would do me no good in Goldfield as I really was not sufficiently acquainted with any business person in that town. So that point was out of the question. The only way I could realize on it was to send it in for collection when I got to one of these cities and that meant waiting a period of possibly three weeks in that particular town before the bank could get the regular returns from it.

It looked as though I was up against it to travel in first-class style. The stage fare to Rhyolite was twenty dollars (I am saying nothing about automobiles) besides the meals and lodging on the way. It then took two days to make the trip. The universal price for a meal was seventy-five cents and lodging one dollar per night, besides my stay in Rhyolite. As Rhyolite was so far from the railroad I knew I could not expect hotel prices there to be any cheaper than intermediate points. Then there was my return trip in the event I did not stay. Fare, one way, $20.00; meals and lodging for the two days, one way, $5.00 to $7.00; besides my stay there and return. I had money enough to take me nicely one way and a few dollars left—but that was the limit.

There was one thing I could do though and save myself the possible chance of being put in an embarrassing position of being stranded. It did not take me long to make up my mind to do that thing, not nearly as long as it has taken me to tell this. I had always prided myself on being an exceptionally good walker. I would "hike" it through and if I did not like the "diggings" I would "hike" it back, asking odds of no one. I hoped no one who might overtake me in any conveyance would offer to give me a "lift"—as I was not starting out to walk to be taken through on "lifts."

I soliloquized this way:—

"A mine was never discovered in an automobile. It is all right for a capitalist to come in later in an 'Auto' and buy the mine but at the present time I am not on a capitalist's footing.

The man who has good legs and is built for walking has an edge over other people in a new mining camp that one cannot gainsay and that he should be thankful for.

The walk will do me no harm, and furthermore it will keep me in trim, as I expect to knock around the hills a great deal the next few months.

I can make from $7.50 to $10.00 per day by so doing, and that looks good to me while I am doing nothing.

I can make forty miles a day thus making the journey in two days—the same time as the stage. Then too I am up against it. There are no two sides to the question. I will walk"—although I would not advise one out of one hundred to make the trip. Mind you I have always prided myself on being an exceptionally good walker. In fact, during one period of my life, I was "champing at the bits" to get up a 500-mile walking contest. I was open to all comers.

So after having breakfast, writing letters and making a few pannings of rock that I had picked up the day before but had not panned as yet, I started out. I made a late start as it was 8:30.

The day was without any particular incidents. There were a great number of freighting wagons on the road and a person could see the cloud of dust they made for miles ahead, so many times I would make a bee-line for the cloud ahead cutting down the distance. The first wagons that had traveled through the desert had picked the way that gave them the least resistance, avoiding ravines, skirting hills, and finding passes over the ranges—therefore the roads that were formed were not altogether straight.

The automobile companies were making a road for their special use, but as it was not entirely finished, they were not as yet using it altogether. The road was surveyed and had cut down the former distance to quite an extent. There was much speculation as to the distance from Goldfield to Rhyolite,—some would claim it was 88 miles, others as low as 77 miles. The automobiles were now making the run in $5\frac{1}{2}$ hours between the two points. Every now and then one would whiz by, and in another twenty minutes it could be seen climbing up a summit some five miles away, go over the ridge and out of view. A telephone line had already been established.

During the day I passed a couple of new watering stations on the road and reached what is known as the Montana station at about 4 o'clock in the afternoon. I wanted to continue, as I felt in trim to go on a few miles further, but there was no other station under 25 or 30 miles distance at that time outside of Summerville and Thorp's Mills (Montana and these other two stations are within three miles). So there was nothing to do but turn in. By stopping at this station I could take advantage of a cut off in the morning, so I would not have to go by the other two.

Water is procured at the Montana Station at a depth of a few feet. The proprietor of the place was an elderly gentleman who had always lived in the northern part of the state, being sheriff for a number of years in his county. He is such a hospitable, energetic old gentleman, that if he ever wanted the honors in Nye County and it depended on my vote to elect him, the honors would be his all right

He also has the reputation on the road of setting the best table, and his beds cannot be beat. There was a colored man who did the cooking, and serving at the table. He made an answer to a question that I put to him, that I'll never altogether forget. His nationality somewhat puzzled me. I knew he had negro blood in his veins, and yet I was almost sure he had Indian blood also—so I asked him if there was not some Indian blood in him. "Yes sirreh—little mixture of everything—Mexican, Negro, Indian, Spanish and I don't know what all else" was his quick response.

At Thorp's Mills, which lies three miles away at the base of the mountain, is an old mining property that has been worked for the last twenty years. While it has been operating under adverse circumstances on account of being in former years so far from a railroad, making provisions and material so expensive, it has nevertheless paid for itself from the start, besides a nice little fortune that has been taken out by its owner and plenty more in sight. It is on the main road of the new automobile line and a telephone station is being installed. Since the time of my passing by there they have platted the land and started a town.

A RAINY DAY

The next morning it was raining. I waited until quite late before starting out hoping it would stop, but as I saw it was in to rain all day, and as it had slackened up some, I ventured out.

Soon after you leave Montana station, ahead of you lays what appears to be a large body of quiet water. It looks good to one to see that in the desert. You wonder if it is formed from springs or from surface water that is shed off by the mountains, which lie on both sides but some miles distance. You think to yourself that it would make a nice summer resort, or, as it looks so white, although it is already summer weather, the thoughts of a skating pond come into your mind, as it resembles one so much. You wonder if there are any fish in it, and if boats have ever been sailed upon it. Your mind is full of such thoughts, but it looks too good to be true. You have to go a few miles and get right into it almost before you discover that the chances to take a plunge, make any fancy maneuvers on the ice, land any whoppers, or go boat riding with your best girl, are very remote on that lake. It is a delusion and a snare. It is so large that one makes to one end of it, for he thinks the only way to get on the other side, is by going around the point. It, however, is not a real lake, just a "Dry" one. It is thought that there was a lake there sometime, and now during real rainy weather, so it is claimed, water gathers, but it soon sinks into the ground, and the deposits of alkali, or borax or some other composition, whatever it is, makes it white, thus causing the delusion.

I helped, or rather tried to, for an hour during the day, one freight wagon outfit that was stuck in a bog, and passed several more freighters mainly all going toward Rhyolite. It rained a good share of the time, while it was as a rule not a heavy rain at times it came down in pretty good sheets. I arrived at Mud Springs, which lies 10½ miles from Rhyolite, at about 4:30; had supper, or dinner, whichever it was, and was going to finish up the trip that evening, but as I met a friend who was there for the night he insisted so strongly on my staying over that I did so. Anyway, by the time I had had supper, and allowed myself to cool off I was pretty stiff. The next morning I took my time in going into Rhyolite, and spent the afternoon of that day in the hills north of the city.

A NEWLY BORN CITY

Rhyolite is situated in what may be called a horse-shoe, for there is an opening on the fourth side which widens out quite perceptibly after one enters the city, and the other three sides are hemmed in with mountains—thus the mountainous rim around Rhyolite is of the shape of a horse-shoe. The enterprising town of Bullfrog lies on the fourth side, or the side at which you enter, at the opening of the horse-shoe, and at the base of what is known as Bonanza Mountain, which is rightly named. These are two cities but as they are building together it can practically be called one—one city with two names and two sides.

The hills in the District looked good to me from the start. I was a tenderfoot and my judgment might not be worth much, but the hills were bright—had life to them and looked as though they were highly mineralized. I had not more than struck the district until I knew that was the place I was going to stick to. The next few days I made it my business, whenever opportunity presented itself, to get other peoples' views. I would always aim to ask some one whom I thought would have no object in telling me anything but the truth. I have not heard one dissenting voice in regards to the hills and many, to put it mild, exceptionally good views.

As the town was young and the influx was just starting, there were many there picking locations for business. The town had three lone tents in the latter part of January, 1905. When I struck it first, three months later, it was a thriving burg of 1,000 souls and I knew within another month 2,000 would not more than count them.

It was a problem to know which would be the best street. There were two business streets that had the buldge over the others and which one would have the supremacy was hard to figure.

The business was all conducted in tents, stretched over a framework of wood and the bottom boxed for a few feet up. There were a goodly number of lodging houses. These were all large tents over a wooden framework. I put up at the best in town. There was a long aisle leading from the front to the rear door, and apartments on both sides of the aisle. Each apartment was separated from others and from the aisle only by a loosely hung curtain of green, strung by wire at the top. No floor in the tent—no chair or any piece of furniture, not even a mirror or a match box, nothing except cots, and there were two of them in every room—one on one side and the other on the other. As there were upwards of twenty rooms, there were fifty cots in the building, and each one was occupied. One could not pick his room-mate but had to take what was given him. He was as liable to be with a horse thief as he was to be with a preacher, or was as liable to be with a preacher as with a horse thief. But as both in the new mining camps of Nevada are as scarce as hen's teeth, it is probable you are not sharing the quarters with either. The regulation price of cots is one dollar per night.

A "HIKE" BACK TO GOLDFIELD

It was upon the third day of my stay and I was taking a "hike" over to another near-by town—Beatty—five miles distance—when in my travels I met a gentleman who was going to embark in a manufacturing business—in a business that I considered was one of the best lines in the section. It was an undertaking I was somewhat familiar with, in a general way, and it took my eye immediately. I stayed with him the balance of the day and before we separated it was understood that we get busy together. I had the privilege, if I so desired—which I did—to put my "mere shoe-string" with his large one, into the business when the proper time came around. As we had to wait for plans and specifications for the building, there was nothing that could be done for the next three weeks. It was arranged that I meet the first consignment of freight at Las Vegas at that time.

Well, I felt pretty jubilant to again get busy at some business I had all confidence in, but I had three weeks on my hands before I had to be at Las Vegas. I would sandwich in a trip to my parents who lived at Riverside, California. I had not seen them since they went west and wanted to make them a visit for some time.

This would be my opportunity, but, my money was lower than ever. Not much, but say a ten spot— (I still carried that New York draft around in my pocket, but this would buy me nothing). Then also my tent and belongings were in Goldfield. I would have to get them first.

I could reach neither one of the boys by wire or by telephone as our camp was out beyond Jumbo, and the service was poor. I thought of writing, but they might be in Lida, for I had written them the day before not to wait, if they were doing so, as Rhyolite looked good to me.

Ready for a "Hike."

I could bank on no one but myself. I told my newly made partner of my intentions of making the visit, and I was to receive a wire telling me the exact date that I was to meet the freight at Las Vegas.

So it happened the same evening that any one in the town of Rhyolite could have seen me, without much cashable money in my pocket, with my canteen on my shoulder, "hiking" back to Goldfield, so as to remove my residence, after which I would make my parents a visit.

I left Rhyolite 5:30 in the evening, walked for three hours, 8:30 P. M. to Mud Springs, where I stayed all night. Walked all the next day making a station five miles west of the summit and a few miles south of "The Tanks," where parties were boring for water. There I stayed the night, and the next day walked into Goldfield in time to get a 2 o'clock Sunday dinner, thus making the distance in less than two days, by over three hours.

A SEARCHING PARTY AVERTED

I showed up at the boys' tent just in time to avert a searching party going out to look for me as they were forming one to start a hunt, when I turned up. From my remarks the morning of my departure they were not surprised at my non-appearance that night, and the following night did not give them any uneasiness, but when almost a week went by, and no word from me, they felt sure that I had gotten into the mountains, sprained an ankle and was still there.

Neither one of the letters I had sent them had been received. The one I sent from "The Tanks" the morning of the third day they never did receive, as was also the same fate of other letters I wrote to other parties at the same time as I have since learned. The second letter they received the following day after my arrival, therefore I made better time than the letter as I put it in the Post-office, at Rhyolite, personally and did not leave there myself until the evening of the following day. They had also received their mail the day I returned as well as the day before that.

It took me a full day to take down my tent, pack my

belongings, which consisted mainly of a folding cot, mattress, pair of blankets, comforter, and some wearing apparel; all of which, with the exception of a dress suit-case of clothing, I wrapped into one bundle, then into the tent.

I made arrangements with a freighter to deliver my bundle and tent poles to Rhyolite for the very reasonable sum of 3c per pound, 110 pounds, or $3.30—that with a few dollars I paid the boys to square my batching account, together with another dollar or two I paid out, made my cash supply still shyer.

I made arrangements with an express company to deliver my dress suit-case, 5c per pound, which was reasonable enough. This express company had just put on a fast service making the trip in one day. They had four changes of horses en route and each change being a four-horse team, making sixteen head in service altogether during the day's trip. They had these relays at watering stations along the line. They would start out with a four-in-hand and push them through to the first station, there make a hurried change and with their fresh four, push them through to the next, and so on to the trip's end.

This service had just been installed and it was also their business to carry passengers. As I could not get the suit-case sent through to Las Vegas, as I wished to have done, and told them to send it to Rhyolite and I would see that it got out from there—they asked me point blank if I intended going through. At first I thought it was none of their business—I might say—"damn business"—so as to put emphasis on it and that was really what I thought, and was reluctant in telling them—but, as I saw they were really anxious to know,—my heart softened and I replied—"Walk it—I can make it in two days and that is pretty good wages for me." "Impossible—Impossible," was one man's reply. I then told him I had made it from Rhyolite up in less than two days giving him the exact time—"and I can surely make it back in two." He then said—"I wouldn't advertise it. That is doing better than the stages and you would make the so-called stage lines ashamed of themselves." I didn't tell him there would be no danger of my letting it out (that was before I ever thought of knocking out this book), nor did I tell him I expected to make Las Vegas (where I would take the train to Riverside), in another three additional days, walking, nor that the twenty-dollar gold piece which I gave him from which he was to take his pay, $1.00, was all the money I had to see me through.

I left Goldfield the next morning again starting to make an over land trip, this time to Las Vegas, a distance of upwards of two-hundred miles. As I was leaving the city I saw the manager of the Fast Stage and we exchanged salutes. He had already seen his stage off.

During the day I had time to admire the mountains, which, by the way, there are some that look good to me and that I would like to prospect some day. They are situated on the right-hand side, at some distance, and if I remember rightly, they are soon after you pass over the summit. I arrived at the Montana Station (I tell you it is the best hostelry on the route) at about sun-down—stayed all night and after breakfast the next morning was again on the road to Rhyolite, which town I reached at 7:30 that evening—thus making the return trip in two days.

Upon my arrival I had a great time finding my baggage which had been sent the day before and had been pigeon-holed some place and I could not locate it until the following morning, too late for it to be sent out on the stage to Las Vegas which left that morning. As this stage south made only semi-weekly trips at that time it would be three or four days before it would again go. As there had been several freight wagons in from the south that morning with cargoes of goods, I concluded to see them as an only resource to fall back upon, as I wished to get my change of wearing apparel to Las Vegas as soon as myself.

I went to a lumber yard—several wagons had come in with lumber—to see a freighter.

The lumber yard was besieged with people wishing to buy that commodity. A wagon would no more than get stripped of its lumber until the load was sold. Men of all sizes and all vocations of life were there—buy their boards, whatever they would need—pay for them and carry away on their shoulders. If they had too many to cart away at one time they would pile them in a bunch at one side and hire some one to watch them until the last piece was safely away from the grabbing—purchasing public. There were also ladies among the buyers. Here would be one that had made a purchase, handling the boards one by one, arranging them into a pile away from the others so as not to get them mixed, watching over them with an eagle eye, as carefully as a hen would watch over her brood of chickens, until her husband, or hired man, would come and carry them away. Or another one would buy a single board—(a great many sales were made where they just wished a board)—pay for it and carry it away on her back. Thus the traffic went on. There was no credit business in this. Here are the boards—pay your money—cart them away—or hire some one to do it for you. Did you ask what was the price—13c per foot, and it had been, until recently, 15c, for plain lumber; a 14 foot board $1.85, 100 of them $185.00, and so on, no matter what the size of your purchases might be.

I saw several freighters. The best time any of them would make the trip back to Las Vegas with their empty wagons was four days besides the balance of that day. I didn't like the idea but I could do no better so had to stand for it. One gentleman that took my eye as being a pretty trustworthy sort of person and seemed to have as speedy a team as any of them said he would take myself, and baggage, both for $4.00. I guess he counted me the same as any other freight, same as a sack of ore, or a bale of hay. While they didn't weigh me I figured it out after-

wards, when I commenced to think of it, that it would be
2½c per pound, baggage, carcass and all. While their
regular rate was 3½c from Las Vegas up, I believe they did
have a reduced rate on the return trip as it was almost all a
one-way freight—very little going back.

You might think that I was tickled to have the proposition made, but I was not. It was entirely slower than
I wanted to go. My idea was to make it in three days,
while now it would take five. True I would have a chance
to ride instead of walk and I had a heel, on which I managed to raise a good blister on the muddy day of my first
trip, and it could stand a good deal of petting. Although
I felt it was as much of a job to spend five days on a slow
freight wagon, as it was to walk, and more so, I would
anyway have to wait at Las Vegas for the suit case to
arrive and that would be as costly and as tiresome as being
on the road, so I accepted his proposition.

They (that is the old gentleman and his two sons)
always kept batch and we agreed that I should go in on my
share of the grub—I purchasing the necessary articles.
They had extra blankets so I had to take none.

I liked the freighter's appearance, and later liked his
acquaintance very much, but I guess he was suspicious of
me, or afraid my pocket-book might be flat, for the second
evening out he asked me for the loan of five dollars. He
wanted to buy a bale of hay or something. So from Ash
Meadows on I was prepaid freight. He afterwards got
some money and paid me the dollar difference.

TWO OPPOSING ARMIES

The freight teams pulled out from Rhyolite about 10
o'clock in the morning and went to Gold Center on the
Amargosa River before dinner, where we loaded up with
water. The freighters all have a barrel on each side of
every wagon for their stock. They always fill these up
and it lasts them until the next well or spring where they

replenish the supply. This is the last water to be seen enroute in the Amargosa River, the dry bed of which you follow down for a distance of forty miles. It differs from most rivers. Instead of becoming larger as you go down the channel it becomes no river whatever unless it has an underground flow, which is more than probably true, as it sinks all of a sudden. Between the towns of Beatty and Gold Center it loses itself and reappears several times. You can walk across its bed on dry soil in one place, while further down the channel, or further up, it is quite a stream. This channel runs quite a distance south, finally winds around the Funeral Range and empties into the sinks of the Amargosa in Death Valley.

During the first day's trip to your left are some mountains with alternate light and dark strata in them, several deep, each strata coming to a V shape, while in advance are peaks that stand out alone but are backed up by this array. These mountains remind one of a regiment of soldiers, first a company of white, then a company of colored or brown, marching in phalanx style, and the peaks that stand in advance—officers of the army.

Here nature teaches a lesson, as one cannot look at it without having the thought of strength come to ones mind. One thinks if they were soldiers how hard it would be to check them in their forward wedge-like advance, unless an opposing army of equal size and as well generaled was making the advance upon them, and then how little chance they would have to cope with these as they have already gained the summit and are apparently marching from the summit down upon the valley below.

There is also something on your other side and across this peaceful valley, a few miles distant, to take your eye. It lies some distance out on the plains at the base of Funeral Range, beyond which is Death Valley. This is a mountain of sand—of shifting sand. I should judge it is four or five miles in length and I have seen it from four hundred to five hundred feet in height. The freighter with whom I was riding said he had made twelve trips past it and had never seen it the same shape any two times. It is caused from the loose sand being blown there. The mountains seems to be arranged just right, no matter from which way the wind might blow, so as to collect this sand at that particular place, forming it into a small sized mountain. But, instead of it being rugged and jagged on the top, like most mountains are, it comes to an edge as if the sand had been dropped through a traveling hour-glass making instead of one peak, a pointed ridge, the entire length of this shifting mountain, besides the by-ridges. Its shape depends on how the last winds caught it, whether they came up from the valley or across the mountains and through the gaps.

While its general trend is always the same, a northwestern—southeastern direction, there are many features about it that change with every wind. How long it has taken to form it is hard to tell. It gives one an entirely different impression than the mountain across the way—instead of showing strength at every point it shows weakness on all sides.

With these two mountains apparently arrayed against each other does the All Provident mean in this manner to give man word that the horrors of Funeral Range and Death Valley can be avenged by the united force of mankind, or this pretty valley, the Amargosa Valley, which lies below and between these armies, as other land in the country becomes worn out and the people more congested, that this hitherto seeming waste can be made fruitful—say through irrigation, if invaded upon by a body of strength instead of a shiftless, reckless people?

Man would care for no nicer place to live than in this valley between the Bare Mountains and the Funeral Range, if it was made productive which I believe it can be. All this valley needs to make it one of the most ideal places to live is water. Can it not be developed? Has not the

Provider of mankind placed an abundant amount of underflow there to be had when the proper time comes? With this rich agricultural valley to live in, with its delightful climate and altitude, surrounded on all sides by mountains rich in beauty as well as precious metals—what more can man ask for?

Man has at last apparently entered this region to live. Will he profit by what nature seems to be trying to tell him and make this valley along the Amargosa productive, as well as conquer Funeral Range and Death Valley which lie beyond?

ASH MEADOWS

The first night we camped on the desert while the next night brought us to Ash Meadows, a little to one side but a nice place to camp.

Here two large strong springs within a yard of each other belch up a large body of luke warm water. The channel of water that comes from these springs is so large one could not encircle more than one-half of its volume with his arms.

There were a great many freighters camping here. They could get free water, buy their meals if they so desired, and also make purchases of canned goods, feed for horses, or almost any commodity in that line.

One freighter who wished to make a purchase said the least he had was a fifty dollar check on one of the firms he was hauling for. The proprietor, a Swede, by the name of Hollenbeck, replied—"That is easy, I have enough in my pockets to cash that and lots more in the trunk." The freighter afterwards predicted, that the man would be looking down the barrel of a six-shooter some day and be demanded to produce if he continued to make such breaks as that about his money, out there in the desert, forty miles from any town.

About six weeks afterwards, one Friday evening after

the freighters had retired near their wagons, out in the open, in their beds of comforters, a lone, smooth-faced man—light hair, stooped shoulders but tall,—entered the store at Ash Meadows made a purchase of some beer and tobacco, offering a fifty dollar bill to be changed.

The little girl waited upon him and asked Mr. Hollenbeck's sister—a middle aged lady who was near—for the change. The woman returned with a box of silver. The stranger then asked for his change in gold, whereupon she entered the next room—a room used as a dining room and only separated from the other by a curtain door-way—proceeded to take some gold out of a box in its hiding place under the floor. She was about to return when she discovered the purchaser was close behind. He struck her on the head knocking her senseless, grabbed a box of silver, another of gold and another of paper from their hiding place—pushed the little girl aside and made his way out under the side of the tent. He had a horse waiting upon which he galloped away.

The alarm was given—freighters aroused and they endeavored to pursue the highwayman but without success. The amount secured was $1,180. Mr. Hollenbeck was away at the time, being in Las Vegas, and his sister and the little girl were temporarily in charge.

INDIAN CREEK

We reached the summit the afternoon of the third day, and from that on to Las Vegas it is down hill. We passed two recently made watering places—Rosey's and Miller's No. 1—before reaching Ash Meadows. They were both wells and were unlike those between Goldfield and Rhyolite, in fact, they have to go a great depth in order to procure water. Soon after leaving Ash Meadows we pass Miller's No. 2, from there on would be the longest stretch in the road where there was no water—a distance of thirty-three miles to Mosquite Springs, a natural one three miles from Indian Creek, although there was a party by the name of Johnson boring for water at a place eight miles before you reach the summit. There are always new stations being formed and the road shortened and so forth. At this time a short cut is being made from the summit in to Rhyolite by a Mr. Miller. He claims he can cut the distance down considerably from Las Vegas in, now it is 129 miles.

One thing I noticed that was very conspicuous after the summit was reached—was the great amount of flowers. There is a cactus that grows in the mountain region of Nevada that is very pretty. It stays in bloom for several weeks and many of them are to be seen in the cities in small tubs, or other receptacles, as house plants and they are very hard to beat for beauty. There are a great variety of mountain flowers and they are as a rule of a bright color and profusely scattered. I should judge there were twenty-five varieties of the more brilliantly colored ones.

Indian Creek is a very picturesque place for the desert—it having some very large trees and a nice spring of water. It is one of the very few old ranches in this part of Nevada and farming has been carried on here for a number of years. There is a reservoir, or rather a fish pond, in which a large shoal of fish can be seen.

After leaving Indian Creek there are two other fair-sized springs, one at Corn Creek and the other at Tula, before one reaches Las Vegas, but neither one is as strong as Indian Creek or Ash Meadows. They both flow a distance then drop out of sight. Ash Meadows does the best—it flows twelve to fifteen miles before it becomes a sub-channel river.

Besides these few oases the country en route to Las Vegas is barren with the exception of grease-wood bushes, which are green the year round, and some sage-brush and the wild flowers, in the early part of the summer. There have been no Joshua trees since about half way between

Goldfield and Rhyolite until the summit is reached, about fifty miles from Las Vegas, where they reappear again, but of a different species and only for a few miles.

The third and fourth night we camped on the desert, while the afternoon of the fifth day we made Las Vegas. One of our party counted the freight teams that we met loaded with freight for the Bullfrog District. He counted upwards of seventy during the five days—that was exclusive of stages and vehicles for passenger traffic— just freight teams. A few outfits had only two horses, the bulk

20-Mule Freighting Team.

of them had four, six or eight and quite a number had a greater number—twenty head being the largest outfit. Seventy outfits—say they average six head to the outfit— that would make four hundred and twenty head the one direction. I presume there were as many coming back as there were going and as six head to an outfit is less than the average it would be safe to say there were one thousand head used for freighting purposes between Las Vegas and the towns in the Bullfrog District. This is saying nothing about those from the north—between Tonopah and the Bullfrog District.

I met a freighter who had made six trips. He started with two fair horses and finally acquired eight head, most of them spanking good ones, two wagons and a trailer. His outfit was worth $1,000 in excess of the one he started with, and besides his own living he had been providing for his family in Salt Lake and had $300.00 to bank. He did this all on a start of a poor two-horse outfit and believed he could easily bank $500.00 a month from that time on—although on account of hot weather he would have to figure on—roads being cut up more—more head of horses to the amount of freight hauled and longer time to make the trip in. Up to that time he had been making the loaded trip in seven days and the return in five.

We arrived in Las Vegas on the afternoon of May 16th. The town up to this time had been in temporary quarters known to the residents there as "Rag Town." This "Rag Town" was about three-quarters of a mile from the regular town site which lies near the depot. "Rag Town" had sprung up to meet the demand until the regular townsite was put on the market and snatched up by the purchasing public. They had at last auctioned the lots off, the day of our arrival, May 16th, being the second and last day. The people bought well and lots as a rule ran high. The purchasers were already wading through the fine dust, made by the freighters in the easily loosened up soil, and were locating their lots in the terra firma below, preparatory to building.

While Las Vegas is as dusty a city as I ever got into, it is not more than fair to give some of its good qualities as it has redeeming features. It has plenty of water at the depth of a few feet. It is a division station on the new Salt Lake Route. That company has established a large round house there; also repair shops. It is a supply point for freighters for a large scope of territory, that is liable to be opened up by prospectors, although it is a few miles distance from any large mountains. The writer has visited the city twice since and the streets were being curbed paved or oiled, and there was being erected a new and commodious depot.

A STRAIGHT TALK

The fare to Riverside, my destination, was $13.30. Of course, it is needless to say that my supply of cash—after paying my passage on the slow freight, my share of the rations for that trip, and subsequent expenses, was inadequate.

However, I had two cards to draw yet and I hoped I would help my otherwise weak hand with one of them. First—I had an acquaintance here but the last time I heard from him, a month previous, his intention was to leave the town on a visit home. After spending an entire evening looking him up, I at last found out for a certainty he had departed a week previous. This left me just one card to draw. There was a very prominent business man located there who had previously lived within five miles of the city where I also had lived for a number of years, in the east. While I did not know him, or he me, I knew people that he knew also. Through this source I hoped to establish my identity. Even if I did establish my identity that would help me out none as far as my responsibility was concerned as I had no letters of credit, not even one of introduction. He would only have my word as to my willingness and ability to pay—and that I was not a smooth fake through and through—only wishing a ten or twenty just because I thought it was policy not to try and get more out of him.

Of course, I was on the line of a telegraph now and could wire friends for money, but that I desired very much not to do. So the next forenoon (the train did not leave until the afternoon) I presented myself to this Las Vegas business man and gave him a strong talk as to who I was, where I had been, and where I wanted to be.

As I knew he was responsible, I told him I had a New York draft in my pocket and I would be more than willing to put that up with his banker in "escrow" for a loan of a few dollars. So after giving him a straight talk, to some length, I managed to get him to take a chance on me and my New York draft for a small loan—I taking a receipt from the banker for the paper. That afternoon found me on the train (the first train I had seen for a month and a half) speeding homeward.

While it was night when we passed through the "Devil's playground"— the full moon was shining so brightly that it gave us a chance to form some idea of the grotesque shapes the earth's surface has in this well named playground.

It is needless to relate in detail the events of the next few weeks. By far the greater portion of my readers know what a visit home to the old folks means. Of course I enjoyed a plunge in the blue surf, the rides on excursion boats and to idly watch the merry makers at Long Beach; Pasadena with its Orange Grove Avenue of elaborate residences and grounds; Red Lands with its Smiley Heights, and also the clean city of Riverside with its Victoria Hill, Magnolia Avenue, and its large orange groves and flowers within the city confines. Also the strawberries and cream, fresh vegetables, and home cooking tasted pretty good to a "desert rat" and took no small part in the enjoyment.

During my stay I had a good chance to go into business and to make it more binding I received word from the party I was going to get busy with in Nevada that his plans had been changed, and it would be some time before his machinery could be installed—possibly several months —as he had to wait upon an auxiliary concern being installed, that furnished part of the raw material. It would be so long before they would be ready that he advised me not to necessarily wait for it.

I had seen Nevada and its possibilities, however, and while California was good to look upon I felt the opportunities were far better in the old grease-wood-state, with its rich mineral resources, than any place I knew of, and I had previously "gadded" around the country a great deal looking for a new location before finally sizing up Nevada. I considered it the best I had seen, so after a few weeks' stay I was again on Nevada soil.

NOTHING IN SHORT CUTS

I received my pay for working in the mine while on my visit. I arrived at Las Vegas one Monday afternoon too late to get into the bank. There was a passenger conveyance going out the next morning at five and another one at seven—neither one of them would wait until after banking hours. The regular stage was going out the second morning, but every seat was engaged ahead. It looked as though I was delegated for a tiresome wait in Las Vegas or again to "hike" it. I also had business to attend to at some of the watering places.

I waited until the bank opened when I redeemed my "mere shoe-string" by paying the fifteen dollars I had borrowed. Got an egg sandwich and a canteen of water and at 9:15 started on another of my cross country "hikes," but this time not necessarily through necessity but for several reasons; first—to avoid a long wait at Las Vegas; second—to attend to business at the different watering places which I could not do by going by stage; third—to save, while I was still unsettled as to my future, the 20c per mile ($7.50 to $10.00 per day) that the stages charge.

The first day's journey was without special mishap. I had received a late start, 9:15, and knocked off two hours too long at Tula Springs. I stopped there for business but the keeper got to talking "socialism" to me and I listened to his argument two hours before I again resumed my journey—not arriving at Indian Springs—the first stop—until the wee hours of the morning.

On the second day's journey I did not fare so well. I had but little sleep the night previous but was feeling in good trim and was making good strides and by the middle of the forenoon I had left other pedestrians, who had started out before I had in the morning, far behind, and by noon I had gained the summit nicely. Here is where my troubles commenced.

In going down the other side of the summit I thought I could see Ash Meadows in the far distance—due west by my compass. I was sure I could see the small clump of trees and it was right near the point of the mountain—where it should be. There could be no mistake about it. I had passed through there and stayed a night on my trip down and while I had paid no particular attention as to how it lay—I could not help but size it up in a general way. Yes, that was Ash Meadows to a certainty. True the general trend of the wagon road bent to the south here, but I figured that was because they had to pick their way down the hill to avoid ravines and it would only be a matter of a few miles before it would again turn northward.

I was stuck on short cuts. I would make a bee-line to Ash Meadows instead of following the road in its circuitous way. I had been taught and had it proved to me in school—I believe it was the first theorem in Geometry—"The shortest distance between two points is a straight line connecting those points." Why not put these teachings in effect? So I took the short cut.

I traveled late into the afternoon before I saw that wasn't Ash Meadows in front. While Rhyolite lay northward, the road here bent southward to a large extent for no other purpose than to get through a certain gap in the mountains that I could not previously see. I saw my mistake, but I was two miles off the road now and to again make it was another two miles.

While Rhyolite extended north why not keep on going

and bend northward and wind up at Miller's No. 1 or at Rosey's Well, that would take me so much nearer to my final destination. I figured—and rightly—that Ash Meadows was way to one side and southward and by the way the crows would fly from the summit to either of the other watering places on the road it would miss Ash Meadows by several miles. By going on instead of turning back and making Ash Meadows I would not only save the four miles but several more. There was a high range of mountains ahead and between myself and the Rhyolite road, but by crossing them I would be all right.

There looked to be rather a low pass over the range from the north that I felt was the proper one for me to take. But as I could not gain it, until late, I thought I had better make for the lowest looking one in front.

It was nightfall before I got to the foot of the range. That morning, besides a canteen of water, I had provided myself with an egg sandwich. I never took anything more on these "hikes"—an egg sandwich and a canteen of water would last me from the time I ate breakfast until I turned in at night. The day had been extra hot and I had drunk freely of water—I had less than a drink left. I had my sandwich which I had not cared for as yet. I mounted the summit only, of course, to find it like so many other ranges—I have seen before and since—that there was another valley to cross and another hill to climb a little higher than the preceding one. I do not know why I had thought this range was an exception. I guess because that low gap I had made for looked to be so innocent at a distance.

If my reader has ever been in the mountains he knows it all better than I can attempt to tell. If he has not the writer wishes to say one thing—"Never attempt to make a short cut across a mountain range, no matter how extraordinarily easy it might seem, with the expectation of ever accomplishing any short cut feat." After you get on one summit there is another one ahead a little higher,

You go down the valley and you gain that summit only to find another one, still a little higher than the preceding one, and so on. It is like a town that is always expecting a boom and never gets it. The inhabitants want something for nothing. In the winter they will say—"It will surely be here in the Spring." Spring passes—no boom—"It will surely come in the Fall." From Fall to the next Spring—from Spring to Fall and so on, always expecting something they seem never to be able to realize.

At about 7:30 o'clock I sat down on a rock and ate my sandwich and washed it down with the few swallows of water I had in my canteen, after which I resumed my journey. Darkness came on. There was a moon during the early part of the evening but it did not last long. Sure the stars were shining, but the light was insufficient so I could not make much progress—across ravines—up mountain sides—ofttimes from boulder to boulder—many times stepping on a stone that would shove from under—if luck was with me, I would gain my feet on these occasions, otherwise skin my shins or bruise my hands. Many a place I would have to climb down several feet using all precaution possible. As I had had very little sleep the night previous I several times laid my handkerchief on the soft side of a rock, used it for a pillow and took a nap for a few minutes.

While the days on the desert are warm, the nights in the mountains are not so. About the only thing I could do was plod along and endeavor to make the best headway I could. While taking these rests I would take out my compass, strike a match, and from the light that it cast I would get my bearings the best I could as to directions. I was not onto the stars as yet and anyway I would get in a valley where I could not see them only straight above.

It was a long night. Going down dales and over mountains—taking cat naps for a few minutes now and then. Comparatively no sleep for two nights—nothing to eat but a sandwich since the morning previous and by far the worst of all put together—no water in my canteen.

On one of my rests I discovered I was in the midst of a bed of mountain flowers. The breeze wafted a fragrant odor to my nostrils. Fear had not entered into my thoughts and I had kept cool headed as I felt that ultimately I would get out all right. The sweet fragrance of the flowers made me wish that in the event I should sprain an ankle, or meet with other mishaps, in my dark, rough journey, that it would happen near a bed of flowers, as I knew if anything did happen in these untrodden mountains no one would run across my remains for months and possibly not for a a year or two.

It was nearly dawn when I finally, fatigued, gained the last summit and a rather high one. I thought it was policy to wait for a short time until day-light, so as to take a survey of the plains below, possibly it would reveal to me the way to get down and I might see a watering station in the distance.

I took a nap. As it was not so cool as during the night I really believe I slept longer than I had in the other two or three naps put together. I might have slept half an hour, but possibly only fifteen minutes. When I awoke it was sufficiently light so I could commence to take my bearings and it was not long before the sun's glow could be seen in the east. As the sun rose and shone on the plains below I thought I could see the sides of a large tent flop in the wind to the southwest—but I was not sure. Foothills below obscured my view of some of the valley to the north. The wash to the south of these foothills looked to be the best and only way of egress.

AT THE MERCY OF THE DESERT

By nine o'clock I was still in the wash and had not gained the other side of the foothills. The day was developing into a hot one. It was the middle of June. I had to take frequent rests as the lack of sleep and nothing to eat was commencing to tell on me, to say nothing of the lack of water, which is the all important thing on the desert. During these rests with my head in the shade of a greasewood bush, I would try to sleep, but could not on account of the heat and thirst. I had no water in my system and had been "spitting cotton" for some time. I finally gained the other side of the foothills and climbed a small knoll, from where I could see a tent to the northwest in plain sight, but it was from six to eight miles distance, at any rate, and my halts were becoming more frequent. On account of hills I could not see what I had thought was the other tent to the south and as it was as far as the one north I decided to make the later.

My lips and tongue had commenced to swell for the want of moisture, and I sometimes wondered if I could speak, or if I could—how plain it would be? I did not attempt to for fear my own voice would scare me, and I also felt that the energy I exercised would make my tongue and lips much drier.

I did not know exactly where the road lay that connected these two watering places, but I thought I could see a large freight team which was apparently receiving its midday feed. I saw I could not make the watering resort and as the freighters always "knock off" a couple of hours during the heat of the day, as it only looked to be a couple of miles, I thought I could gain him before he again resumed his journey. I was to that stage where I had commenced to "see things" and anything that looked like water close by, I was willing to make for. I was also commencing to become forgetful. The last two stops I made I had upon again taking up my journey left some article behind. Once I had left a couple of pieces of "likely" looking rock, which I had clung to all night, and another time I had left my handkerchief and a pair of cuffs with buttons attached. I was still enough of a tenderfoot to wear cuffs. At last I saw that the supposed freight wagon was a clump of Mosquite brush further on, but I could see the road and finally made it—knowing it would only be a matter of time before some one passed.

Here I lay down as I had done a dozen times within the last few hours, with my head in the shade of a grease-wood bush, such as it afforded. As it was midday and the sun was high, the shade was rather thinner than it had been. There was a breeze but I was too near the ground to receive much benefit from it. This semi-shade seemed to give me more relief than I could get otherwise for my parched swollen lips and tongue. As the shade would shift I would also shift my position. I looked up the road and down the road but could see no vehicles in sight. As a rule this was a much traveled road, but apparently, all traffic had on this particular day suspended.

A couple of hours—I should judge—slowly dragged on—still no freighters in sight. The fates seemed to be against me. I knew if they did not appear soon in the distance none would reach me that night as they would make camp before getting to me. Several times I had attempted to move on, but would go no distance before I was looking for shade. Finally it got so I would not make over a hundred feet on these attempts before I would be looking for shade and the frailest excuse of shade would do. I would drop down on the ground and put my head in under these slight bushes. This was the greatest relief for my thirst. My legs seemed to be strong enough, but the sun would get the better of me. I thought after the evening came on I would be able to make the station all right.

I had been lying in the shade cast by the twigs of one of these smallest clump of grease-wood bushes for some time, when finally, I heard the puffing and exhaust escaping from an automobile as it came cutting its way through the sand. I staggered to my feet and made for the middle of the road so as to intercept it. As luck would have it they were coming to a halt anyway and as they came slowly puffing up I waved my hand for them to stop. I told them "I am all in" and as I saw an empty seat or two added, "Must have a ride. I have money to pay for it." As they stopped I asked for water. I promised them I would only take a swallow or two for a starter and meant it when I promised—but, when I got that canteen to my lips the water tasted so good I forgot about the swallow or two. They took it away from me though and would not let me drink too much. In another few minutes they allowed me some more, under their supervision, and finally allowed me larger drinks.

I engaged passage of the chauffeur, to the next station and tried my d—est to engage it all the way in but to no avail. I put up the best talk I knew how—would pay him handsomely for it. I had plenty of money. Believed it would change my luck to go into the camp in style, etc. But, I could not budge him one iota. He was just making a trial trip. Did not wish to over-load. Had turned down passengers at Las Vegas. One machine went in that morning—if it got there it was the first that had made the trip from Las Vegas without a break down. The roads were exceptionally bad. I told him after the few miles stretch of sand we were in they were better from that on. He did not mind the sand we were in if he positively knew they were no worse, but as he had never been over them he wouldn't take another passenger for any money. Tried the best I could but to no purpose. I paid him two dollars and fifty cents for taking me up to the station, six miles, and felt as though it was the best money I ever expended. The drinks of water I got were worth several two dollars and a half. The only thing I regretted was that I could not engage passage all the way in. Heretofore, I thought I would walk into the camp and ride out—possibly in my own "auto." Now I wanted to ride in and stand the risk of walking out.

In a few minutes we arrived at Miller's No. 1. The other station below, that I had seen in the morning from the mountain, was Ash Meadows.

It was about 4:30 o'clock when we arrived there. So I should judge it had been a good twenty-three or possibly twenty-four hours since I had had a drink, outside of the very few swallows I had when I ate my sandwich at 7:30 the previous evening which was almost twenty-one hours before. The egg sandwich was all I had eaten since an early breakfast the previous day.

No one really knows what it means to be without water on the desert on a hot summer day—one of the longest days in the year—for several hours unless he has been there. As far as hunger was concerned—I didn't mind that as I wasn't hungry, but I thought I never would fill up on water.

The next morning I resumed my journey on foot making Rhyolite early in the afternoon on the fourth day out from Las Vegas, thus being on the road an additional day more than I should, and having the idea—"Nothing in short cuts across mountain ranges" thoroughly branded into my mind. The fastest stages with several changes were making it in two and one-half and three days at that time.

When I was within a few miles of Rhyolite I could hear the continuous blasting going on. The bombardment-like noise from the mountain sounded good. It was the first I had heard for a number of weeks. It makes one realize he is again in the New Eldorado of Nevada. The land of many rich mines. Where the poor man of to-day may be the possessor of millions to-morrow.

During my three trips between Goldfield and Rhyolite and also the trip from Las Vegas—that I have mentioned in this chapter—the only ride I had was the one mentioned —six miles.

I have done quite a bit of traveling since. I have traversed over that portion of the state that, up to date the whistle of a steam engine is unknown—in all upwards of two-thousand miles. I have taken stages where they were convenient, but where they were not—I would "hike." A few places stages did not or could not go—"to hike" was the only alternative.

PRINCIPAL DAILY EVENT—STAGE ARRIVAL

What is the principal daily event of the camp—did you ask? I should say the principal daily event is the arrival of the stage. But, when I say that, it is speaking too generally though, as there are several stages a day coming in besides automobiles and other vehicles carrying passengers, baggage and freight that is sent by express,

Six-Horse Stage.

and the greater number of these conveyances come and go without any special interest to the general masses.

What I should have said is the arrival of the stage from Goldfield, carrying the United States Mail. As there is no direct daily mail service from the south established at this time, the forepart of the summer months, this stage practically brings in all the mail from all parts of the world. It arrives in the evening late enough so the day shift has had time to have their supper and come up town, also the prospectors get in from the mountains and also the numerous miners who have camps established a few miles distance but call Rhyolite their post-office address. They are all there, or their representatives, on the principal corner of the town, waiting its arrival—in hopes of getting a letter from the dear ones at home, or from their old-time chum, or a newspaper chronicling the world's events, or an overdue letter in regard to some important business deal.

Did you ever live any length of time over one hundred miles from a railroad, where you only got to hear of the outside world periodically? If so, you might know what the arrival of the Mail stage means in a new camp of 2,000, situated away from any railroad in the desert and in the mountains. Not that the 2,000 people are not content with life way out here in the hills, for they are. But you'll have to admit, my city reader, that the arrival of the mail means more to us than the arrival of mail if we were living in a large city where several mails were coming in every hour of the day, where we got several deliveries daily, where we could get some penny newspaper, regular or extra, the ink not dry yet, most any moment, or where we were at all times within a few feet of a telephone or telegraph service. Such is the difference, so that, when this particular stage comes in, it is of general interest to all. If it should be a half hour or an hour late, the crowd that has congregated in groups in the streets and in the business houses commence to get restless—"I wonder what is the matter with the stage?" "It has been a sizzler to-day, it pert near tells on the horses." "They must have an extra load."

At last it is seen coming up the end of the street. The driver gives another crack of his whip to his team of four, or six, which is already coming at a full trot, and in another minute the stage rumbles in and mail bags are hurled off. As this stage is well loaded with fast freight, there are but few passengers and they are covered with dust from top to bottom. They alight, the baggage is unloaded, the merchants have some one there to receive their bundles of ice, which they pay 10c per pound for, Goldfield weights, (that is, they stand the shrinkage of the trip), and the fruit commissioners are there to receive their daily order of fruits. Thus it is not long before the stage is rid of its cargo.

In the meanwhile the man who runs the "Corner Grocery" and has been acting as Post Master for the camp, until some appointment is made by Uncle Sam, has sorted out the letters from the papers.

The crowd upon the street, upon the first appearance of the stage, left stories uncompleted and business unfinished, and all commenced to saunter towards the "Corner Grocery," so as to get good positions in the crowd. The next half hour is consumed in hearing the newly arrived letters called for. Upon hearing your name an answer— "Here"—will result in having your letter handed from one person to another in the crowd until it finally gets out to you. One person will sometimes represent ten or twelve different people. Thus the distribution of the bulk of the mail is speedily made. The balance will be left upon the counter for those that are not there, or represented, to come and look it over at leisure.

Upon getting out on the street again you can hear the newsboys calling out their daily wares,—The "Denver Post;" "Salt Lake Tribune;" "San Francisco Examiner," "Bulletin," "Call," "Chronicle." Any of these papers you can get for 10c a copy. If it is Wednesday night one will be able to get a Sunday morning San Francisco paper —they are four days late but are the first in the field.

Later on during the summer a regular post-office was established. Mail was also received daily from the south coming by the way of Las Vegas. But the calling off of the evening mail still stayed in vogue until the stages, on account of the heat, commenced to run nights, arriving in

Rhyolite in the morning instead of the evening. Postage stamps, at times, have been hard to procure in camp, and pennies are unknown.

A CHARACTER

"Happy" and the piano player from the Dance Hall can be seen staggering down the middle of the street arm in arm. They have made the rounds of several saloons and have a fair-sized jag on.

The first time I saw "Happy" was in the Dance Hall. He was attired in a pair of blue overalls, hung so loosely over his hips that I could hardly see how they managed to cling over his frame. He had his right hand in his hip pocket which he could not much more than reach, his blue flannel shirt—much the worse for wear, too long in the sleeves, and fastened by a string in front where the third button should be, hanging loose and blouse-like over his waist—was tucked into his pants with very little margin to go on, and in some places less than none, where it hung loosely over them.

On that first occasion, when seen, he was standing in the middle of the floor—the music had stopped, the girls and fellows who had been dancing were at the bar drinking, while a few others were seated around the spacious room. With that right hand in his hip pocket—hardly reaching, and from which I should judge from the pockets bulged out appearance contained all his worldly possessions,— while he drew his left hand over his face, wiping his nose. His hair was disheveled, a two weeks' unkempt beard was on his face, and with his one remaining eye,—his right one, which looked as though it had cobwebs on its blinkers,— he was looking wistfully at the bar as if in hopes to hear some one say "Give 'Happy' a drink."

I did not know who he was at that time, and did not see him for several days, but afterwards I learned that he had been put under arrest by the constable immediately after the ball game the next day They allowed him to see the game through before taking him into custody. The offence was chicken stealing, and he was supposed to get thirty days, but was back on the streets within ten days. Instead of taking him up to Tonopah, they had kept him at Beatty chained, with other prisoners, to a wagon wheel, and let him loose after ten days for good behavior.

Since his release he was to be seen every day on the streets. He was one of the odd characters of the town, and as he was a base ball enthusiast, he was always at the games. If any one should ask him if he were enjoying the game, he would answer with a Sol Smith Russell slowness, but with more of a nasal sound, "W–e–l–l, I w–o–n–d–e–r i–f I d–o–n–t. I k–n–e–w K–e–l–l–e–y o–f B–o–s–t–o–n, t–h–e b–e–s–t m–a–n t–h–a–t e–v–e–r s–e–t f–o–o–t o–n a d–i–a–m–o–n–d. I w–a–s b–o–r–n a–n–d r–a–i–s–e–d i–n B–o–s–t–o–n. I l–o–s–t o–n–e e–y–e l–o–o–k–i–n–g f–o–r w–o–r–k. T–h–e–r–e i–s w–h–e–r–e y–o–u g–e–t y–o–u–r g–l–o–m–m–i–n–g–s."

None of the old timers in the Bullfrog District will ever forget his sayings, as he was quoted by the majority of the people in town. It wasn't so much the sayings, but that drawling manner he would say them in. Among the more frequent ones could be heard: "W–e–l–l, I w–o–n–d–e–r i–f I d–i–d? W–e–l–l, I w–o–n–d–e–r i–f I d–i–d–n't? W–e–l–l, I w–o–n–d–e–r i–f I w–o–u–l–d? W–e–l–l, I w–o–n–d–e–r i–f I w–o–u–l–d–n't? I w–o–u–l–d–n't s–a–y t–h–a–t t–o y–o–u."

AN AFTERNOON AT HOME

As one sits in his tent he hears blast after blast as rounds of shot are fired in one of the numerous mines, situated in the adjacent mountains which are hugging the town. These blasts are quickly followed by their echo through the mountains on the other side. The echo much resembles long peals of thunder, and one not accustomed to it will think a storm is approaching, only to look out upon a blue and entirely cloudless sky. He has only to wait a few moments until other blasts are heard. This time it is from the mountains that previously gave back the echo. This time the other mountains return the salute in their prolonged, thunder-like rumblings. The town instead of being called Rhyolite could just as well answer to the name of "Echo" and the mountains to the name of "Thunder Mountains," but the rhyolite has always been here, while the echo has only come with man,—thus the "prior claim" which stands for much in a mining camp.

From the south side, or Las Vegas way, a gust of wind has gained speed in coming up the valley. It is cone-like, and brings with it dust made by the freighting. As it goes up the main street of the town it gathers fragments of papers, which are snatched up and twisted high into the air. It rattles tin cans together, turns the empty beer bottles around, and proceeds on its way, apparently to lose its force and be lost sight of as it approaches the mountains on the fourth side of the town. So strong a gust of wind may not occur again for a week, but generally a fair breeze comes up before midday, making the weather quite agreeable, especially if one can get into the shade.

These are not all the noises; besides the blasting, the echo, the rustling of the tin cans made by the wind, there is the flapping of one's tent, the buzzing of the fly, the swing of the ax of a new residenter, who is staking down his tent, the sawing of lumber and the sound of the hammer on all sides.

There is a wagon rumbling by. It might be a jobber's wagon, or it might be a water wagon. You look out. It is the water wagon. You have the privilege, by hailing the driver, of getting a barrel refilled for the small sum of two dollars, or, if you wish it in smaller quantities, unless you find a too independent driver, your canteen filled for ten cents. It takes fifty head of horses to supply the people of Rhyolite and Bullfrog with water daily. The teamsters get the water at springs three miles distant for twenty-five cents per barrel, or at Beatty, four miles distant. Some of them haul seven or eight barrels to a load, one or two of the wagons are equipped with regular tanks. They make one and two loads a day each.

Other people are boxing up their tents, also workmen at $8.00 per day and with $130.00 per thousand lumber, are constructing much needed accommodations, one of which is the new hotel, the Southern, only two stories high, but which will cost, it is said, $20,000.00. It is within a block of the writer's tent. There are several laborers at work rapidly bringing it to completion. Another is the new hospital, which lies within a block on the other side. While there has been very little sickness as yet, the energetic citizens, or rather the charitable ones, the ladies of the city and the Miner's Union, who should receive especial mention, are seeing to it, that everything possible is being done to look out for the welfare of the district.

There is also the crowing of your neighbor's rooster, the cackling of a hen, or the long braying of some jack, besides the continual travel of pedestrians, generally singly but occasionally in pairs,—the loose fragments of rock which constitute the upper soil grinding together underneath their feet. Several passers-by have sacks of ore which they are taking to their individual tent to pan and see if they can get much "color," or, if they wish to be more sure about it, they take it to their assayer. They come from all parts of the mountains lying back of the tent.

All these and a great many more sounds come to the writer's ears as he sits in his tent on a June afternoon in the residence section of Rhyolite.

MILES' AND BROWN'S STORIES

It was 10 o'clock, but I felt it was too early to retire, so I told my friend that I was going to walk around the block first to see if there was anything extra exciting going on.

It was an evening in the very last of June. While the day had been hot, it was now cool and pleasant. There was not the usual excitement, as so many of the residenters had gone out the last few days to spend a few weeks in Denver, San Francisco, Los Angeles, or some of the beaches. There was more or less excitement though, but nothing special on tap, and I was about to go to my tent for the night when I, by chance, ran into a couple of prospectors whose names were Miles and Brown. Prospectors who come in from the outside are always interesting—possibly these had been to some of the more recent strikes—and one can get a more authentic report from them, so I tarried.

They had been prospecting in Funeral Range for the past several weeks, and only came in this time for one of them to get a pair of shoes, as his footwear was entirely worn out, and they were going to return in a couple of days. They thought well of Funeral Range, and said it was highly mineralized, and believed there would be a big rush for that section as well as other parts of Nevada, the coming Fall, Winter and Spring They said they figured that if they kept on during the Summer months they would be that much ahead, as there were very few of the prospectors but what were "knocking off" during the hot weather. They had located a couple of claims that carried values, but had struck nothing that assayed big on the surface.

As they had been in Funeral Range, of course the conversation soon ran into "Mysterious Scott," "Death Valley Scott," or as our friend Dyer had called him, "The Burro Man." After "Mysterious Scott" was broached once, the conversation did not lag for the next two hours, but we could not solve the mystery as to where his fabulously rich mine was located. That he had a bonanza "graft" somewhere, we all had to admit, as there were several there to vouch for his being a lavish spender,—they had met him on the outside where he spent his money recklessly. It was true he would go broke occasionally, after which maybe you would see nothing of him for a while, but he would soon be popping up again and spending money as lavishly if not more so than before. Who was he, and what did he have? Why hadn't people been able to find his mine? All these questions and more too, we discussed. They were as much bewildered as I.

Brown said—"He is surely a mystery. Sometimes I do not see how he can have a mine in the Funeral Range, and yet he must have. We have been up and down the Range for eighty-two miles, and while we weren't looking for Scott's mine," so Brown said, "but we were prospecting, we couldn't see the least sign of a trail. Burros would leave quite a trail, but we didn't even see a man's footprint or an upturned stone. Some say he pads his burros feet as he enters Funeral Range so as to leave no trail. Mind you, we weren't looking for Scotty, but we were keeping our eyes open all the while. The Range, as a rule, is very abrupt from Death Valley, and there are only a few places man can get up. If Scotty has a mine there, I do not see where it can be. I know I did not cross any trails or see any footprints, but those that I know where they led to. Yes, he is a mystery that will be solved one of these days. We have our own assay outfit that we keep at the Furnace Creek Ranch. The Ranch for the last nine months has been run by an Englishman by the name of Lennt. Scotty also has always a change of four burros there, but Lennt knows nothing more about where Scotty's mine is—if he has one—and he surely must have—than we do. He has a change of burros there—he has other changes in different places, one change at Daggett, I believe. He comes and goes. Lennt says 'When he goes in he hasn't any ore, or at least you cannot see it—when he comes out, he exhibits ore and in a short time we hear of him in Los Angeles or elsewhere spending money like a millionaire.' No, we never met him face to face, although he was there one evening when we were, not over a fortnight ago. He came late and left early. Lennt told us in the morning 'Scotty paid me another visit' and there were different burros than were there the night before. We heard him during the night when he came."

Miles said,—"Lennt, the party who runs the ranch, is no one's fool. He is one of those fellows you can bank on what he says. Lennt asked Scotty at one time why he didn't record his claims, that he should think he would want to for protection. Scott's reply was—'Locations can be misleading and still hold good. The work shows for istelf.'"

Brown said "Scott has a group of twelve claims on record. They are all described lying due east of Bennett's Wells. He was grub staked at one time by a New York man who is his present partner. Bennett's Wells, as you know, are on the west side of Death Valley. It does not say whether they lie five miles due east or one hundred and five miles. He must be an eccentric sort of a cuss, as I do not see what he gains by keeping his mine a secret. Another thing,—his every act is known almost up to the time when he leaves Furnace Creek Ranch, and enters Funeral Range. It is known where he was last night, where he was the night before, where he was the night before that. He camps at such and such a place one night, some other place on the desert or in the mountains say twenty-five or thirty miles distant the next night, and so on. It is no secret, as every prospector and rancher, while they are few, keeps cases on his movements. The news travels from one to another. After he leaves Furnace Creek,—his camp fire can be seen in the Range the first night out at a distance of about twenty-five miles,—then all track is lost, the same as if he had gone up in smoke. He is not heard or seen anything of again until he returns with his burros laden down with ore. I am told he was arrested once for train robbery,—that it is a matter of record in the Courts. The story is something like this: The Santa Fe train was held up, and the express boxes rifled of a very large sum of money, somewhere on its main line, below Death Valley. Scotty right after that was very flush and had exhibited large rolls of money. Suspicion rested on him, and he was arrested for doing the deed. He let the trial go along and it didn't seem to worry him any, but finally when it came down to a pinch, and he was asked how he got his money, he showed the Court a bill of shipment for ore and its returns. He also at one time had a working partner;—his partner was missing. Scotty, it is said, was also arrested for murdering him, but nothing could be proven against him. Scotty says his partner went out with $4,500 worth of ore and hasn't been seen since."

Another one of the group said he knew Scotty in Goldfield during the winter. To show how eccentric he was, he said he was with Scotty one day when a man approached them and asked Scotty if his name was Scott. Scotty answered him by saying—"Scott, did you say? No. My name is————," using some assumed name. The man replied—"Well, I am mistaken. I thought you were Scott," after which he departed. Scott then made the explanation—"What is the use of telling him my name? I don't know what he wanted. He might be a deputy sheriff looking for me." "And that seems to be his nature right through," added this acquaintance. "He always keeps some one guessing."

The group of us discussed the pro and con as to who Scott was, and where he got his money, for quite a while, there on the corner on that June night, and we came to these conclusions:

He has an abundance of money, at least spasmodically, if not at all times. He also makes frequent visits to

Death Valley and Funeral Range, and he also has changes of burros, in small groups, stationed at different places at all times. These above facts are known about him.

How he got his money we imagined was one of four different ways:—

First:

He has a fabulously rich mine, as he claims, more than probably located in the Funeral Range.

Second:

He has money coming from some other source than a mine, but is prospecting in Funeral Range, and being an eccentric number, is continually misleading the people. (We thought there was nothing in this second guess, but of course there is the mere possibility.)

Third:

He holds up trains or express companies, etc., making very large "killings" occasionally, and uses Funeral Range and Death Valley as a blind.

Fourth:

That he is a high grader (that is, one who steals rich ore), *and is in cahoots with the manager of one of the old properties that is being worked, and they are fleecing the company,—he taking the rich ore, or greatly reduced ore, out on burros to railroad, and afterwards dividing the spoils with the manager. The property might not be in Funeral Range or near Funeral Range, but he makes Funeral Range and Decth Valley to "side-step" the people.*

We all agreed he would not be as much of a mystery in nine months from now as he is to-day;—that will include the Fall of 1905, and Winter and Spring. If he is, he is a good one.

The author of this book is thinking very seriously of

going down there and ferreting out the mystery of the location of the mine himself, and incidentally try to locate some good claims.

RHYOLITE'S FIRST "FOURTH"

The evening of the third of July witnessed a throng on the streets. The miners had come in from the hills on all sides and were congregated in groups exchanging views. All were enthusiastic over the prospects in the different sections.

Most of the business places were decorated with the National colors. Several of the more patriotic ones had secured spruce trees, which grew about eight miles distant, and had had a row of them placed in front of their places of business.

The large stone for the drilling contest on the morrow had been placed in the middle of the principal cross streets, and who would win was the conjecture of the evening.

The thirst-quenching places in the city of which there were some fifty all did a thriving business.

There were no fire-crackers allowed on account of risks of fire, but it was evident that celebration was going on.

While we were over one hundred miles from a railroad we got the Hart-Root fight for championship, by rounds, which was being pulled off at Reno. One of the drinking resorts had made arrangements with the new telegraph company for that service.

The morning of the "Fourth" was a hot starter for a day, but it did not seem to lessen the ardor of the celebrators or the enthusiasm in the least.

Nine o'clock witnessed the Grand Parade with Judge Ray, Marshal of the day. It was headed by ex-senator Stewart and party, followed by the fair ladies of the town in conveyances and floats, after which "Death Valley Slim," a notorious prospector with outfit, brought up the column, closely followed by the Miner's Union, in large numbers, and then other citizens of the town, to the extent of several hundred, brought up the rear singing national, patriotic and comic songs.

The next and greatest event of the day was the double drilling contest. There were five entrees:—Ray Bros.; McD—— and McElravy; Donely and Banks, of the National Bank; Tenny and Martin of the Mayflower, at Crystal Springs, and Campbell and Ross.

As each pair stepped to the platform, stripped of everything but undershirts and overalls, ready for the fifteen minute fray, they were greatly cheered by their followers. These outbursts of enthusiasm, loud applause, and shouts of encouragement kept on during each performance. A great amount of betting was going on but after Ray Bros. finished their fifteen minutes without making hardly a single fumble, or losing a stroke in changing, or in their shift of drills, and had 47 5-16 inches to their credit— it was even money—Ray Bros. against the field. McD—— and McElravy did some good work—one was good at turning, while the other was an extra strong hitter. When time was called they had made $44\frac{1}{2}$ inches but Tanny and Martin did better work in changing and finished, hitting strong, with 46 5-16 inches drilled into the rock. The other two pair did not do so well, both making about the same time. The first money, $350.00 and entrance fee, was captured by Ray Bros., while the Crystal Springites took the second money, $150.00.

After dinner there was foot racing galore,—the ladies' race; the fat men's race; girls' race; boys' race; potato race; etc. Besides horse racing, one-half mile, best two out of three; one-quarter mile dash; slow burro race, one-half mile, riders changed; ladies' nail driving contest and many other features.

During the horse race, one-half mile, best two out of three, in the first heat two horses became unmanageable, jumped the track and made for their barn with the riders.

After bets were placed against them they came out first in the next two successive heats—one taking first money and the other second.

The young lady—who was a runner—and won first money in the ladies' foot race, also won first money in the nail drilling contest, in a walk away with several competitors in the field. She then turned around and offered to bet a bunch of money, at a ratio of one to five, with a man that she could beat him in a foot race. It was accepted—money put up. She won.

The evening was taken up by a patriotic, and well appreciated speech from the honorable ex-senator Stewart, who represented Nevada in the United States' Senate covering a period of forty years, and who has taken up his residence in the Bullfrog District. This was followed by fireworks from the top of Bonanza Mountain, and a grand ball given by the women of the new hospital for the benefit of that institution.

These were not all the events of interest. Many were filled to the brim, until their feet would not track any more, and not a few fistic encounters were mixed in, for diversion, during the day and night, in this usually very peaceable city.

In one of these fistic encounters, the one who got more than he gave the other fellow, said he would not take revenge then as there were too many against him, and he wouldn't get fair play, but if he ever caught him out on the road, single handed, he would settle with him. A deputy sheriff who had been instrumental in separating them, and keeping them apart, said—"If that is how you feel about it—you'll have it out with him right here. We'll make a twenty-four foot ring—referees will be chosen and you can fight to a finish, and we'll see you do get fair play." The officer made a diligent search for the other party for some time so as to bring off the mill, but he had previously gone home or elsewhere and could not be located.

As the sports were too much for one day, the celebration was continued all during the fifth of July. The big event on that day was the single handed drilling contest between Ray Bros. and another pair of drillers. It was to decide a bet, $1,000 a side. Ray Bros. landed the $2,000. This event, with a ball game, and many other features filled in the day. Thus went the first "Fourth" in the Bullfrog District.

A TENDERFOOT'S DISAPPOINTMENTS

A young tenderfoot meets with many disappointments in looking for gold. He does not get acquainted with how

A New Strike.

it should look or act, until he has panned "color" five or six different times. Once he gets a string of gold, he will never get gold again without knowing it, although he might still make pannings and think he has it several times when he hasn't. There is something about gold that is different from all other metals—while it is slow of speed it is alive in color.

First a young prospector should catch on to the motion to give a pan. The specific gravity of gold is so great that it is natural for it to remain in the bottom by giving the pan the right motion; also on account of its weight it is slow of motion, bringing up the rear in his greatly reduced pannings. A young prospector should always pound up his rock fine—not use so much rock but get it in as fine a powder as he can. He should be sure his piston, mortar and pan are free from gold dust before starting in, otherwise he is liable to "salt himself."

He should get acquainted with as much rock as he can. Familiarize himself by seeing the ore from the different mines and make frequent pannings. In this way he will get in touch with "likely" looking rock.

At first he will not know what kind of rock to look for, that will be liable to carry values and cannot tell quartz when he sees it—consequently he will pan "every old thing." This is a good fault though, as "gold is where you find it." A kind of rock that does not carry values in one section of this vast country is liable to in another section and visa versa. Many a good property has been overlooked by an old time prospector, just because he was too all "cock sure" that he could tell by the looks of the mountains in general, or the rock, that there were no values there, while a tenderfoot would stumble along later on and discover what would subsequently, with development, become a big mine. Cripple Creek can be sited as one of these cases. Coloradoans say that a great number of gold fields in Nevada resemble, in many respects, Cripple Creek.

By far the greater number of Nevada's finds have been a free milling proposition, consequently the ore generally can be panned, but where there is any doubt it should be assayed, as some properties that run exceedingly high in values are hard to pan—especially can this be said where it is a talc substance.

Another thing a young prospector—or rather a tenderfoot—tries to do, is to find a gold mine with the gold just sticking out of it, right on the surface of the ground—not even as low as the grass roots. He has seen ore from some of the mines that was "lousy" with the yellow stuff, and he thinks a mine isn't worth having unless he can at least see gold in it. He will soon find out differently but still he will continue for a while to keep one "eagle eye" open for rocks with nuggets in them, from the size of a pin head, up. I know when I first started to work in a mine and the rays from my candle light would strike a crystal or mica formation just right, so as to make it sparkle, I thought—before I had given it an examination—I had struck gold sure, and there was many a minute during the day when I didn't give my employer "value received"—trying to find him a gold mine.

One occasion I believe I'll never forget altogether. That was when I thought I had a good show of finding a gold mine for myself.

I hadn't made many trips out in the mountains, in fact, I had been working all the time, when one day I was going across country. I was in the flat lands about two or three miles from any mountains when I saw a rock that contained gold sure, I believed. It was a dark red rock with specks in it. It looked to me at that time as if it couldn't be anything else but gold. These specks were of a brass color but yellower, and with the sun shining on it I thought it was free gold, yet I had found it so easy and the gold looking like specks were so large that I was not sure but that I might possibly be mistaken. While it was only "float" in the flat away from the mountains, I felt as though I could easily trace it up and find the ledge. That was what I was going to try and do the next day.

I took my bearings. It happened to be to one side of, but near, a telephone or telegraph line that had been surveyed. The poles were not in yet, but they had stakes every few rods and each of these stakes bore a number of its own—thus I had something to tie to. By tying my handkerchief, which is still there, to a grease-wood bush, I marked the place where I had discovered the float. By getting in a bee-line between the telegraph stakes, with the aid of my compass getting in such a position on that bee-line, so the handkerchief, or marker, would be in an exact northeasterly direction I was commencing to get my bearings. I marked the spot that was the intersection of this bee-line and this northeasterly—southwesterly direction line, by a bunch of stones. Then I commenced to pace it off—and take my notes. So many paces from the stake that bore such and such a number towards the next stake. Then go in a due northeasterly direction so many paces, I believe it was 166. So as to put a check on it and have more than one thing to hang to in distance, I still went on in that northeasterly direction until I came to the wagon road—210 paces more. I also got the number of paces from the bunch of rock to the other telegraph stake. It was on a bee-line between a small peak (next to large peak, north) in one range of mountains on one side, which were at a distance of a couple of miles, and the middle of three large black points, or projections, in the range on the other side, some several miles distant. While I was getting this location down pat for just float, which had been carried for several miles, I felt as though it might behoove me to do so, as it might aid me the next day to ascertain, by the aid of the washes it was between, from which mountain it came from. Whether it was from either of the ranges on the side, or from the third side where there had been some rich mines struck. I put my notes down so that I could be sure and read them, but that other people would have a hard time to decipher them in the event they were lost—or stolen. I also thought of having another copy and put it in another pocket as a precaution against losing the data. I knew that after the assays were made, it would leak out somehow that I had discovered something—either through the assayer (I beg assayers' pardon) or through myself, as I felt as though I could not hold my enthusiasm unless it proved not to be gold. I also knew that it would take me a week, or possibly a month, to find the ledge where it came from. I wanted to be the first to find it, as I was sure, if that was gold—and I wasn't sure it was not—it was either a Breyfogle, or,—"The Lost Mine of Three Peaks," or one just as good, and I did not know exactly how I would "side step," to use a Scotty phrase, all the people. I left the handkerchief where it was but removed the bunch of stones, so in case my notes should be lost there would be no pile of stone there to help tell the tale in case of being found.

After getting to the camp I borrowed a mortar and piston and went after the part of the rock that had a few of

Pounding Rock.

these large specks in it. I had already panned other people's rock, a couple of times that left a string of yellow in the pan. I was disappointed in mine not showing up as it should, but there still might be gold in the pan as the general rock was of a reddish nature any way, so I asked three or four people if there was any color in it. They all told me the same thing—"nothing." Not being convinced exactly I showed them the rock and what I thought was gold.

A couple of other tenderfoots, in the grocery, thought it was the same, but the old timers told me how I could tell that it wasn't.—First, it did not have exactly the same brilliancy any way you might turn it, while gold would have; Second, after being put in water it didn't have as much color as before, while water would have livened gold up; Third, my specimen had a smooth flat surface while gold would probably not have. None of the old timers laughed at my judgment though. I guess they had been there before. I didn't tell them how much trouble I had gone to to get my notes on the location, or of the thoughts I had been entertaining as to how I would evade all the people until I located the ledge from which the rock came. I wonder if any of them ever thought they had discovered something when they hadn't. I dare say every one of them has been through the same mill in their early mining life.

When a young miner really does feel good though, feels like jumping in his boots with glee and give an Indian war-whoop—is when he really makes a panning and gets plenty of color on some property that is his own.

"SCOTTY, THE SCOOTER'S" TRIP

It was but a few days after the evening spent with Brown and Miles in Rhyolite, before the newspapers all over the country came into the camp with news of "Scotty" being in town—Los Angeles—and spending his money lavishly Column after column, in these various newspapers, was devoted to this "Man of Mystery" and his high flying. They told of his tossing a roll of greenbacks into his wife's lap that counted up to $175,000 for her use as pin money; of his putting up at a hotel in the city, of his getting disgusted with it, and going over to another where he engaged another suite. These were two of the leading hotels in the city. Of his having money in all pockets, and of one-thousand dollar bills being his hobby, and of his wanting to make Chicago, or better still New York, in a record breaking and almost impossible time. He was in no hurry to start to the "Windy City," but after he did start, he wanted speed and plenty of it. He had money to pay the railroads for transportation and didn't see why he could not get it in as big chunks and delivered to him as he wished, the same as any other commodity.

In another few days the newspapers came into camp stating that he had made arrangements with the Sante Fe to be delivered into Chicago, from Los Angeles, in the hair raising time of 45 hours. He had wanted them to go better than that, but they would not consider faster time for any amount of money.

The fastest time previous to this was the "Peacock Special," which created quite a stir. The time made then was 57 hours and 58 minutes. This would be slicing that down almost thirteen hours, but the ex-yap-of-a-cow-puncher and Buffalo Bill ex-champion Rough Rider was not satisfied even with a 45 hour run. While he had the yellow stuff, it was evident he had no sign of a yellow streak running down his spinal column. But as the Sante Fe officials stood pat on this time, he finally engaged a "Special" to make it in 45 hours, which by the way is going at no burro pace. He did succeed in getting a concession in his favor though. He was to pay them $5,500 for the "Special" and if they would make it in better time than the 45 hours, he would pay them $20.00 per minute for every minute they would slice off—and they in turn to pay him $20.00 per minute for every minute they required over the time.

With the above conditions, the record breaking "Special" cut out from Los Angeles at one o'clock (Pacific Time) of the afternoon of July 9th and arrived in Chicago amid a throng of people the second forenoon at 11:54 o'clock. Time 44 hours, 54 minutes—6 minutes better than the contract.

This lad-of-a-man of mystery of Death Valley and Funeral Range had broken all records from Los Angeles

The Monte Cristo of Death Valley

to Chicago by 13 hours and 4 minutes. The train made the last 239 miles from Fort Hamilton on, in 244 minutes, with Charles Losee, Engineer, at the throttle. During the trip it is said to have gained as high a rate of speed as 106 miles an hour. As this train had the right of way the entire distance, he practically owned the track while his train was in sight.

At Chicago he put up at the "Great Northern," where he held "open house" in western style. He was besieged by would-be-promoters and schemers of all sorts, who wanted to enlist him and his millions into their enterprises, but he let it out cold that he was buying nothing but speed. He did get landed for something that a "desert rat" should not have been landed for. That was a tailor-made suit—the first he had ever had—provided it was delivered in four hours. Upon his arrival in Chicago he was attired in coarse lace shoes, hand-me-down pair of pants, blue flannel shirt—collar attached, red string tie and soft felt hat. No coat or vest.

In buying speed "Scotty" tried to engage it on to New York in thirteen hours time. It was thirteen hours or nothing. As none of the railroads would make it in that scandalously low time, "Scotty" had to be content to take the regular eighteen hour train.

While "Scotty" wanted to make it to Chicago in quite a bit less than the 45 hours, he had to admit, that the time made was "rambling some."

Thus this freakish man—this young-man-of-mystery, who has kept us all guessing the last few years, wended his way across the country. And this already much titled man won for himself another name. Besides being known as the "Burro Man," "Mysterious Scott," "Death Valley Scott," and plain "Scotty," etc., he is known, for the time being, at least, by the additional name of "Scotty, the Scooter."

—DOVES—

We have our beautiful things here the same as elsewhere. Doves are numerous. While they are very plentiful there is more prejudice against shooting them here than in other places and very few are shot. Man feels as though they are a welcome pioneer of the country, the same as he himself—a forerunner or messenger of cheer, so to speak—consequently not very many are slaughtered. If every person that enjoyed eating fresh game, would commence to slaughter these at the beginning of the season, it would not be many seasons before they would be completely exterminated.

Later on, during the summer months one cannot go out in the hills hardly, unless he scares up one or two that are nesting. They flutter out of the bush—half flying, half hopping, along the ground, feigning that they are crippled, keeping just far enough away so as to lure one —who is not on to their game—on, away from their nest of two white eggs. One will follow them for several hundred feet in the endeavor to catch them, when they fly away as well as any bird.

Whether they came with man, or whether they preceded him, I cannot say. Anyway they have the same instinct to protect their young from man here on the desert —where man did not tread during their previous nesting season—as they have elsewhere.

RATTLESNAKE STORY

There are a great number of grasshoppers here, and there is also another insect very much like a grasshopper, in fact I guess it is a species of the same family. It makes a noise very similar to that of a rattlesnake. This insect stays on the grease-wood bushes, and, being of the same color as these bushes, and not moving around much, it is hard to detect. One not knowing what to look for, might look in a grease-wood bush several times to find out the cause of the rattle, and then not be able to locate it. They are practically in every bush though and these bushes in a great many locations do not average over three or four feet apart. I know I looked several times for the cause of the rattle before I could locate where it came from, not on account of its not rattling incessantly, but because it was exactly the same color as the wood and I expected so much noise to come from something larger.

This insect's fifth and sixth legs are many times larger than any of its other four—the same as a grasshopper. When these legs are not in use they are folded up hinge-like along the side of its body, thus resembling wings. The vibrating of these wing-like legs, by hitting on its back—or otherwise, I could not determine—which the insect does quite frequently, causes the noise. But, what I started to tell you is a story about this "rattle."

I have an acquaintance who had been to Nevada some two years before my arrival. This was before Goldfield, the Bullfrog and the other new districts were dreamed of. He had to go overland 70 miles in order to get to Tonopah. Afterwards when he was telling me about it and how he had missed the chance of his life by not staying there, he added—"My but rattle-snakes there are something awful. They are as plentiful in the desert as flees are on a canine's back. At first I didn't know what they were, they were so thick."

I should interrupt my story here by telling you this acquaintance was an albino—one of those oddities of nature—with a head of hair as white as white as can be, and pink eyes that he could hardly hold open on account of the light.

"They are on every bush," he said, as he looked sideways towards me, squinting his eyes open the best he could, to see if I was there. "They wind themselves around the branches of the bush. I did not notice them at first until my attention was drawn to them. Yes, I would have made big money if I had stayed there. I had one mining property offered me for $800 that has since then been worth its millions. But I would want to make big money though to want to live there—nothing but a desert and rattlesnakes."

After I got out to Tonopah I met one of his friends. I mentioned how this party had said there were so many rattlesnakes there, when this friend had to tell me how a party of them played a practical joke on this fellow, making "White-head," as they called him, believe there were rattlesnakes, and that they were coiled around the limbs of the bushes. They became so serious in their conversation about it that he really believed it—in fact, they got him to open his pink eyes in the sunlight, which was glaring to him, wide enough so he could see them, or imagine he did, coiled around the bushes, and he hasn't known the difference. "He was game though; while it rather made him shudder because there were so many of them, it didn't seem to phase him much. We have never given the snap away to him—and I never thought of it before as he seemed to be pretty cool headed—but I presume that is why he never located here. He evidently hasn't forgotten. There being a few rattlesnakes around here made the play that much stronger, as he mentioned it to one or two outsiders, but got no satisfaction. About all they would say was, 'I 'low a person might run across one if he stays long enough.'"

TOWNS OF THE BULLFROG DISTRICT

As I have somewhere before said, the town of Rhyolite is hemmed in by a rim of mountains which resembles a horseshoe—with Bullfrog at the opening of the horseshoe. But that is not the best of the story, these mountains are very highly mineralized. While not all of the best properties of the District, lie in the immediate proximity of the cities of Rhyolite and Bullfrog, so many of them do that this community can hardly fail to be anything but the metropolis of this district. On your right-hand side, as one enters the city, is the Ladd—Benson mountains which contain the Ladd—Benson property, National Bank Mine, and many others,—further on, but still to your right and in front, is the Montgomery Mountain—which holds among other properties the great Montgomery-Shoshone Mine, while on the left is the rich Bonanza Mountain—containing the Gibraltar, Eclipse and Great Eastern Mines and numerous others, every one of which is

Freight Team Loading Ore.

a good one, and further over, the Denver—another very good property.

Thus, the hills that surround Rhyolite are hard to beat. The Original Bullfrog and the Gold Bar lie still further west, and may be cited as among some of the best in the District. The Mayflower, which has a big outlook, lies around Crystal Springs some seven miles north of these cities. The Royal, Lonsway, Lige Harris, and numerous others, lie nearer Beatty and Gold Center, to the eastward.

The cities of Rhyolite and Bullfrog became a city of 2,000 inhabitants by June 1st, 1905, where they were composed of but three tents the last of January, 1905. It remained a city of about 2,000 persons during the summer months as canvas life on the desert is not the coolest life. But as more frame buildings are erected, the writer predicts, and he wishes to be conservative in so doing, that the time is not far distant when 10,000 will not number them. When he says 10,000 within a short period he means in Rhyolite and Bullfrog, which are practically one. A great many predict this, and it looks as though they are justified in so doing, that is, to be the largest city in the state in due course of time.

Gold Center lies on the Amargosa River about four miles east of Rhyolite at the base of the Bare Mountains. From its geographical location, it lying in the midst of a good mineralized section, also being the natural junction for the railroads that are building into the country; also good location for mills, it is predicted by a great many level heads to be a city to take second place only in the Bullfrog District.

The town of Beatty lies one and one-half miles north of Gold Center. It is also on the Amargosa, and in turn, has its admirers and enthusiastic citizens.

BIRD'S-EYE VIEW FROM FAIR VIEW PEAK

From Fair View Peak, which lies east of the Amargosa, can be seen the four towns of the Bullfrog District, all of which have come into existence within the last six months or a year. Previous to the finding of rich ore in the mountains there were three white and Indian families of Davis, Howell and Beatty, who lived on the Amargosa. Their nearest neighbors were forty miles distant at Thorp's Mill on the one side and Blacks, an Indian family, on the other. (These nearest neighbors were in turn isolated from the rest of the world.)

From this point of view,—Fair View Peak—and looking towards the setting sun, on your left can be seen the town of Gold Center, further on and more directly in front can be seen Bullfrog and Rhyolite, while due west but closer, at the base of this mountain and two or three miles distant, is Beatty.

A green streak can be seen reaching up the Amargosa Valley for several miles. Otherwise the mountains are full of color but barren of vegetation with the exception of the grease-wood and sage bush and also the further exception of Indian Springs, which lies to the westward several miles where another, but very small, oasis can be seen.

South of Gold Center the channel of the Amargosa still continues but it is waterless, only a yellow streak to show where it should be. The Amargosa Valley below that town widens out into a nice lying tract of land, several miles in width, extending from the Bare Mountains on one side to the Funeral Range on the other. This semi-green valley is the same hue, except where the river bed should be and a few white streaks, showing a wagon road from Las Vegas and also a newly made path to the Funeral Range.

HORRORS OF DEATH VALLEY

Death Valley and Funeral Range are still entitled to hold their names—given to them years ago on account of the perishing of so many emigrants—and will continue so, if prospectors do not give up the idea of prospecting this region during the summer months as a few have attempted to do this summer, 1905.

I have interviewed several of the old timers who have crossed Death Valley. One old prospector said if a person considers his life worth six-bits he has no business to attempt to cross Death Valley during the heated summer. Another prospector, whose acquaintance I made, was in town under medical treatment for his eyes. He got into the Sinks of Death Valley where it was so hot he burned his eyeballs. Another one says he would not consider crossing it for any amount of money, while another one says he has crossed it at all times and is going to do it again this summer, but one should pick his way and be prepared. In all I have interviewed a score and *as a man* they all say it is a fool-hardy piece of business for most any one, that they are taking their lives in their own hands and it was the universal opinion of all, that it is no place for a tenderfoot during the heated period.

If one has an ample supply of water—and that means just what it says—ample supply, nothing less, then the chances are far more in one's favor than otherwise. So in case he does not find the spring he is looking for, or that it has gone dry since he visited it the month before, that he still has plenty of water left. The lack of water has been the cause of many a lost life. They think they know where there is a spring—in fact they know they do, they have been there before. They have plenty of water to take them. When they get there the spring has gone dry, which many of them do during the summer. Their water supply is exhausted. They are left to the mercies of the heat and the desert. Nobody knows what it means to be without water with these conditions staring him in the face until he has been through it himself and no pen will ever be able to describe it so the reader will be able to live it over in his mind.

My reader may think "O! Fudge! Show me the man, the able bodied man, even if he is out of water who cannot make fifteen, twenty, twenty-five, or even thirty-five miles to water if necessary." That is all right to lay down by a spring, under the shade of a tree and talk, but it is an entirely different matter when you are out of water and on the desert. Many a person has given up and perished when they were within two miles or less of water.

It is peculiar but it is true, if one has water with him he does not get nearly as thirsty as when one is out and doesn't know exactly when he will be able to get the next drink.

The water is not the only factor in Death Valley that should cause one to avoid it during the summer. Many a corpse has been found with a canteen beside him half full of water. The heat is so intense that it has its list of victims also. The water anyway becomes so heated that it is of little service to any one to satisfy thirst.

A great part of Death Valley lies below the level of the sea, in fact, very little of Death Valley proper lies above and some parts are, as Government statistics will show, as far as 300 feet below sea level. Then on each side is the high range of mountains—the Funeral Range on the east, or towards the Nevada side, and Panamint on the west. These ranges have peaks in them, almost hugging Death Valley, that are over 6,000 feet elevation—Mount Smith, 6,300 feet; Mount Leconte, 6,580,—in the Funeral Range —besides several other that are still higher that lie in these ranges only a few miles back—Pyramid Peak, in Funeral Range, elevation 6,750; Piato Peak, Panamint Range, 7,267; Telescope Peak, Panamint Range, 10,989. With this abrupt change of elevation of from less than nothing to over a mile in height, on one side, and in some cases, on the California side, over two miles in height, with the sun's hot rays beating down, who can expect anything but heat—heat unadulterated.

That is not all about Death Valley. When it is wet, the ground is of a slimy, mushy composition, wagons will mire in up to their hubs—and at places it seems to have no bottom. In dry weather this becomes hard, white and dazzling to the eye. The greatest borax works in the world lie in Death Valley and the dust of this together with the soil causes this white composition.

Those who have gone through during the summer months claim one cannot see 100 yards in front of himself on account of the dazzling soil and the very dense blue air that is continually rising from the ground caused by the almost intolerable heat.

At Rhyolite while it may be cool and comfortable

there on account of the elevation, at any time during the summer one can look southward across the few miles' stretch of valley, and see the Funeral Range veiled in this blue air that has come out of the valley beyond.

There is little doubt that the Death Valley region is rich with precious metals but prospectors cannot do much during the dry summer months, even if they had assurance that they could stand the heat. Instead of looking for minerals they would spend their time, and more than probably their lives, looking for water.

There are but very few consecutive days that pass during the extremely heated summer months but that someone is picked up in Death Valley in a deplorable condition, either out of their head or exhausted with the heat.

Here are three cases, where more than probably three prospectors are dead and the survivors in each case didn't have much margin to go on. The survivors of these three cases all got into this one camp—The Bullfrog District, at the time of the writing of this story—within the last week.

The sum and substance of one, as told by John Mullan, the survivor, is practically as follows:—

A party of three, composed of John Mullan, Morris Titus and Earl C. Weller, the latter two brothers-in-law, home Telluride, Colorado, and ages twenty-nine and twenty-five respectively; started out from Bullfrog, June 20th, on a prospecting tour to the Panamint Range—across Death Valley. They had with them nineteen head of burros and two saddle horses and first went to Wood Camp, a distance of twenty miles, where they expected to find water. They found the spring had recently dried up so they redoubled their tracks as far back as Mud Springs. Upon leaving Mud Springs they were told where they could find a water hole in Death Valley. Upon breaking camp the next morning, they only had twenty gallons of water for themselves and their twenty-one head of stock and the water hole to locate yet. They went down a canyon as directed but could not get out and as they got out of water in the meanwhile things commenced to look serious. Finally about 2 o'clock in the afternoon they did come to a moist place where by digging out a hole they could catch about a cupful every four hours. What did that mean when they had themselves and so much stock to look out for. Mullan and Weller stopped, but Titus pushed on so as to look for a few hours longer for the water that they were directed to. He told them he would be back at the camp for the night. He never came.

The next morning Weller took the stock, two of the burros saddled, and started out to look for Titus and water. Neither one has been seen since and they are thought to be dead, as Weller had no water in his canteen when he went out and had no food, as they left all provisions at their last camping place, also several of the burros three or four weeks later came back to one of the springs above Rhyolite a few miles.

The next morning after Weller left, Mullan went out to look for his partners but got sun-struck and lost himself. He wandered about the balance of the day and far into the night before he finally wound up at his camp, more dead than alive. He became so far gone this last day that he had to resort to moistening his tongue and lips with his urine.

He made several attempts at various times to get out of the canyon and locate his partners, but he was so weak, both mentally and physically, that his attempts were all unsuccessful. Finally a fortnight later, a Mexican happened along and brought him back to Bullfrog where he became able to relate his story. He said the heat was intense and his suffering indescribable.

At one time when the three were together, while they were going down the canyon, the burros refused to go. They turned around several times and wanted to go up a by-canyon. Another prospector, who was a few hours behind them noticed the place where they had had trouble with the burros. He afterwards was relating the incident and said if they had gone up the by-canyon, as the burros desired, that they would have found water as there was a spring up there, and it was more than probable they would be alive to-day. The burros had never been over the ground before as they had just been brought here from Colorado by Weller and Titus. The two horses died within the first few days out.

The second story is this:—

A German, Gerard Schaeffel, and wife were camping on the east side of Funeral Range but desired to go to Furnace Creek Ranch, via Death Valley, so as to put their horses out on pasture. They were warned, by friends, against attempting to go at this time of the year, but, regardless of that, they started out with their two packhorses to make the trip. They arrived at Keane Springs all right but after leaving there their troubles commenced. Their supply of water gave out, but they kept on going as far as they dared to in hopes of finding other springs. They could not locate them and finally turned around and attempted to get back to the springs. They became so exhausted that they let the horses loose but finally got back to the springs after being without water for nineteen hours. The man fainted three different times on the return trip and, but for the assistance of his wife, would surely have perished. The horses returned to the springs still five hours later, but their dog dropped on the wayside and hasn't been seen since.

The lady says she can go where any man can, but a million dollars would be no inducement for her to again attempt to make the trip under the same circumstances.

The other story is this:—

Two carpenters by the names of Jensen and James Riff went out in the mountains near Death Valley They were camped at a spring and prospected out from there but one day lost it and ran out of water. They finally got within about four miles of the camp when the larger one—

Riff—gave out and refused to continue. The other one succeeded in making the spring and afterwards went back for his partner but he had gone. Jensen then came to town, a distance of fifty miles, arriving at midnight and together with a couple of friends of Riff's and a team immediately returned in search for his unfortunate partner.

They found places where he had been lying with his head under grease-wood bushes, so as to keep out of the sun. One place where he had been lying quite a while they could see his prints in the sand where he had shifted his position around the frail bush, making a semicircle in his endeavor to shade his head as much as possible from the sun's hot rays. The last signs they were able to discover of him, were footprints, and as they were a goodly distance apart it looked as though he had been running at the time. The footprints showed he was making towards the middle of Death Valley and of course the search would have been fruitless from that on.

Old timers say these thirst-driven-mad men after they get to a certain stage, the first thing they do is to strip stark naked and commence to run, afterwards they drop down on the sand and vigorously paw into it, like a dog.

Jensen says before he left, Riff always wanted to go in the wrong direction and the way he eventually did go.

These are only a few of the incidents where there are survivors left to tell the story. This is just a little over a week's mid-summer record for Death Valley. In all of these cases, the survivors returned to the camps of the Bullfrog District within a period of less than ten days time. How many more cases where the survivors managed to get to other localities, to the west or to the south, is hard to tell, or how many more unfortunates whose bones are bleaching in the sun, where there is no one left to tell the story is still a harder matter. It is estimated that thirty or forty have given up their lives to Death Valley this summer with the season not more than half over.

Steps are being taken by several of the cities of southern California to lessen the deaths in prospecting Death Valley, which lies in California, and their other desert lands. The main thing they will do is to discover all the good springs and have permanent sign-posts placed along the trails directing one to these watering places. Also to discover the poisonous springs and mark them such.

There are numerous springs, but it is an easy matter for a person to get within a half a mile of a spring in this mountainous country and if they don't know it is there—to miss it.

MID-SUMMER VISIT TO DEATH VALLEY

Since writing the above article the author has visited Death Valley. It was during the month of August. The conditions there are fully as bad as have been described.

It is no place for a tenderfoot, or any one else, during the summer months, and this cannot be emphasized too strongly. It is a fool-hardy piece of business.

I got through all right though, and now it is only an experience in my book of life. I am a chance taker but let it be enough to say I would not take the same chance over again—same conditions and everything—for any amount of money. One million dollars—cold cash—to take the same chance would be no inducement whatever; I would not give it a second thought.

Of course, I could not take the same chance again, if I so willed, as I know more about the exact lay of the land than I did on my first trip.

I realize after it is all over with, that it is putting it mild to say that it was as liable to have terminated otherwise as the way it did. I might say the chances were nine out of ten in favor of the other fellow, and then keep within the bounds of conservatism.

During the trip I could have said "I cannot make it—I cannot make it. I might as well give up," and it would have been the very easiest thing to have said and to have done,—instead of—"I must make it. I must make it. That water will taste good when I get there. I must make it."

If I had allowed gloom, despair, and fear to have entered my mind, instead of continually keeping bright thoughts before me, it would have been different.

As I crossed Funeral Range I could not help but think of Scotty's mine. It is the opinion among many conservative men here that Scotty has a mine. Where it is located of course is not known. Funeral Range looks as though it might be just such a place as would have several bonanza mines in it.

If Scotty hasn't a mine, he should have. If not a "Breyfogle" or a "Lost Mine of the Three Peaks"—he should have at least a common, everyday, Nevada mine.

I had Death Valley scene before me all afternoon as I wended my way in a circuitous manner down the steep slope on the Death Valley side of the Funeral Range, gradually getting nearer the base. As one looked over that vast expanse that lay before—engulfed with thick blue heat that continually rose from its desolate bottom—one would imagine he was looking into that region, Hades— into Hades, with the lid off.

This valley that lay before me—this Valley of Death— which has so many victims to its credit—was the valley I was going to penetrate on the morrow. Penetrate for no other purpose, on that August day, than in the interest of science—"What fools we mortals be."

It was mid-afternoon when I sighted a group of tents pitched far below, in the recesses of a canyon which lay to my left. Somehow I had missed Keane Springs in my journey and this was the camp of the Keane Wonder Mine which I saw from that height above. I was in hopes I could replenish my water supply here.

I arrived at the workings before I did the camp and

as it was a tunnelling proposition I penetrated several of the workings as far as I dared to without the aid of a candle. I halloed several times to see if there was any one in the mine, but my call brought no response. I afterwards wended my way to the camp, but found it had been abandoned for the summer. There were no occupants in any one of the seven tents. I discovered there were no springs in the canyon and I afterwards learned they had to pack their water from Keane Springs, a distance of six or eight miles. I had water in my canteen, it being about one-third full, but I wished to refill it here. I found the large galvanized tank which contained their drinking water but the scum which had formed upon it was very thick, showing that the camp had been abandoned for several weeks if not for several months. Although not in Death Valley, they are in so close proximity to it, it is impossible to work these mines only in the more favorable months of the year.

After making a thorough investigation I continued down the canyon—where I found a couple more tents. A dead dog lay by the side of one tent. I recognized the dog as one belonging to a Mr. Harman—so this was Harman's Camp. I had met Mr. Harman, in fact we had had dinner together one day, when he was in the city some six or more weeks before, and the dog accompanied him on that trip. The dog's past master was nowhere to be found. There was no sign of life here. As it was getting dusk and I had discovered a well beaten trail leading up over the higher land, I thought it behooved me to continue my journey. As the path was so distinct I felt as though it led to Keane Springs.

MEN OF THE MOUNTAINS AND THE PLAINS

I had gone about a mile and a half when I saw that the path would soon come to an abrupt end as there was a high straight up-and-down wall of a mountain reared in

The Monte Cristo of Death Valley 113

front. I was some little distance from the wall when I heard a couple of men's voices. As they heard me approaching along the pathway one of them called out— "Hello! Who's there?" "A friend," I responded. "Lost too, are you?" "I don't know. It all depends on whether this is Keane Springs or not." "That's what I thought. Lost too. You are in the same boat as we." "I don't care especially, whether this is Keane Springs. I am satisfied if there are any springs here"—I said as I came nearer them.

They had made a search for water, but there were no springs in the canyon. When they struck the path they thought it led to Keane Springs but after getting here they saw their mistake. Keane Springs was on the other side of the Keane Wonder Mine and they did not see how I could have missed it in the afternoon. It was the only place in the whole section where there was water and that was the place they had intended to make for the night, but had by mistake side-tracked themselves. There were a couple of tents here. This was Driscoll's camp, but, like the camps in the other canyon I had previously left, was abandoned for the summer.

These two men were the first persons I had seen during the entire day (the next day I met no one) and it was just by chance I had ran across them. By their becoming lost, or rather by both of us becoming lost, we had met.

While there were no springs there, they had found some water in the tank. They personally knew that the water had been there for at least five or six weeks as there was no one at the camp at that time. How much longer the camp had been deserted and still how much longer the water had been standing there they did not know. They had previously tried some of it during the evening by giving it to one of their burros and apparently it had had no bad effect and it might be all right for one to drink. They considered it far better than no water. After seeing the thick scum on the water at the Keane Wonder Mine I felt "leary" of it. The cover of this tank could not be removed so an investigation was out of the question.

When they found I intended to make a trip through Death Valley they tried their very best to discourage me. But as they saw I was determined they gave it up. I was discussing the advisability of continuing and taking the chance by night instead of by day—as I was not sure of the water—when one of them—the spokesman of the two—with a quick flash of his eye and with his husky voice spoke up—"I would not let even a dog start to make that unknown trip to-night, let alone a man. I would shoot him down first."

While he put it in a sort of general and diplomatic way, for a man of the plains and the mountains, he could not have drawn a bead on me with his gun and commanded me direct and impressed it more plainly that he meant it for me. He said it in such a way that I knew he meant every word of it too. Besides his husky, matter-of-fact voice, he had an eye on him—some people would call it a bad eye—that showed he would shoot if the emergency justified that stringent measure. At that time I thought it was rather severe talk but my experiences during the next thirty hours changed my mind. It was only necessary talk—and it would have been the most humane thing to have done if it had come to a show down. He knew full well that no man could have made it under such circumstances.

One thing was decided in my mind though, that was, that I would not continue that night.

In a short time we all went to bed and I for one was soon sound asleep. If I lost any rest during the night it was not on account of being with strangers—men of the mountains and the plains, those who could shoot if the occasion demanded it—as they had shown their hospitality and nature more than once in our few minutes acquaintance. I also have no doubt but that my meeting them saved my life.

The next morning found us up a long while before dawn. After participating in a hurriedly prepared breakfast of cakes and bacon and coffee, with the boys, putting up a couple of bacon and slap-jack sandwiches, for my midday lunch, and filling my canteen with the questionable water, I bid my acquaintances adieu.

Upon my departure, while we felt pretty well acquainted, they had stuck to the habit of the country—they had not asked me my business or my name, not even my western name—or I theirs. I have known people for three or four months in this western country—would see them daily—and still I would not know their name or know any one else that did.

I redoubled my tracks of the night before as far back as Harman's Camp, from which place I went down the slope. While Harman's Camp is only about one mile from Death Valley—one has to go three times that in order to get down the precipitous side of the range—it being impossible to go direct down the canyon.

I had been told of a well at the foot of the range, and at the mouth of the canyon, as one enters Death Valley, where one could refresh himself. While the water is not good to drink it is nevertheless wet and one can use it to good advantage moistening his flesh. I would avail myself of it.

The boys, soon after my departure, packed their burros and after a long day's trip made Rhyolite about 10 o'clock that evening. There they told a group of acquaintances of my intention of making a Death Valley trip that day.

So that night while I was struggling in Death Valley with the heat, for my life, there was at least, as I afterwards learned, one prayer that went up for my safe deliverance.

DEATH VALLEY

Before entering Death Valley from the Funeral Range one gets a good bird's-eye view of it. It looks to be one seething mass of heat—the blue air arising straight upward from the surface, from all parts. Small red, or brownish, ridges can be seen here and there—as if made from some volcanic upheaval, or formed by ocean waves. As you look further on, and more into the valley proper—it looks, very much, similar to the delta of a river—white streams can be seen—here it is all in one, there it widens out into several, only to convene again. One must not take this for water—as it is not. It is either borax, lime, or alkali, one, or all, or some other composition—I will not say what. The entire valley is void of all kinds of vegetation—not a greasewood bush, or a bunch of sage brush, is to be seen anywhere.

As you enter Death Valley, and get well into it, you find it is all it seems to be. Perspire during the day—you do not; the heat licks it up before it gets to the surface. The heat tries to dry the moisture out of your eyes—you cannot keep them open.

As you walk along squinting your eyes open occasionally you see a large rock in the distance—there, there is shade—that is your goal for the present. Upon arriving you take a rest as you are tired. You fill the stopper of your canteen with water, from which you moisten your lips well. You also drink a swallow, or two, from your canteen.

After a few minutes rest you push on to make another rock, and shade. Again you moisten your lips and take another few sips of water.

Finally you come to a vast expanse where you can see no rocks in front of you. While you started before dawn in the morning it is now nearing midday—the heat is intense. If you have any common sense whatever you'll not attempt to make this vast expanse but will while away a few hours in the shade.

During your trip you have not seen an animal, not a reptile,—not an insect,—not a bird. Not a living creature of any kind. No flies to bother you.

The heat is so intense you can almost hear it sizzle—that tingle in the air is the only sound perceptible.

You lie there with your eyes closed and pass the hours with comparative comfort. Once when you open your eyes, as you lie on your back and look up into the sky, you see a bird—one of the larger variety—high in the air above, and at some distance. It looks as though it is going to attempt to cross the valley—it is out from the Funeral Range side and is headed westward. You watch it in it's flight. It gets out some distance into the valley, there makes a half dozen large circles, as if undecided what to do. You continue watching it soar in the air as you wish to see the outcome, but, finally it turns back and returns from whence it came.

After the sun commences to settle down towards the high range, on the western side, you again feel safe to continue your journey.

You have been cautious of drinking water but it has availed you nothing—you have no more than enough to make a slush in your canteen.

You trudge along, the crisp soil giving from under your feet. Your canteen has been empty for some time and you thought you had sufficient for two such trips. Empty as much through evaporation, caused by the intense heat, as through what you have drank. One's system gets completely out of moisture. The hot, dry, air breathing over one, as from a furnace, regardless of the sun having set several hours before—then it is, when one's system gets devoid of moisture, that this air seems to take all the vim and mettle out of one, and it is only by great effort, indescribably great effort, that one manages to trudge along mile after mile.

You pass by a newly made grave, which lies to your left, at the side of the road. It holds the earthly remains of Tim Ryan—an old time prospector—who has succumbed to the heat only a few days previous—and has been given a prospector's burial. You kneel on the grave and offer up some sort of a prayer—you can do no more—you can do no less. Bob Ingersoll would have done as much under the same circumstances.

Thus you trudge along hardly able to drag one foot after the other, hour after hour, taking several necessary rests. Upon resuming your journey after these rests you still feel thoroughly tired out. Many times you feel as though you cannot possibly continue and you want to remain where you are lying until you get rested, but you know the results too well. While it would be by far the easier thing to do you again after a while gain your feet and stagger along.

During the evening you have removed your clothing a time or two, in the effort to get some relief. While it is scant you have hardly enough energy to replace it. Your canteen, weighing only a few ounces becomes a heavy burden to you but you know it is the best friend you have and you will not part with it until you part with life. Many times during the day you have hugged it to your breast and have been as saving as possible of its contents while it lasted. Oh for some more water or a refreshing breeze instead of this furnace-like blast of heat. Dismay enters your mind. You soon see that will not do. You change your thoughts and look forward only, to life and hope. You are saying in a whisper to yourself—"I must make it. I must make it. Life is sweet. That water will taste good when I get there. I must make it." Repeating the same sentences over and over again you continue staggering on.

At last you come to the Old Borax Works. You had not heard of them. There must surely be water here. Furnace Creek must surely be near. You cannot hurry, so you consume quite a bit of time groping around—first on one side, then on the other, behind the office, out towards the barn, then through the works by the old tanks and vats —trying to find something tangible—such as a house, well or a green spot where there might be a spring. Then you go through the large office building, lighting matches to guide you. But no water can be found.

After a long wait in the endeavor to get rest, you continue your journey. The road must lead to water— water must be beyond. Finally you hear the barking of a dog in the distance. It is as if grabbing for the last straw and being successful. It encourages you.

How you get to the stream you hardly know. You do not run. You can scarcely walk. You sit by the bank and think how thirst-satisfying even is the sound of its rippling. You take your first drink, then soon another and another. You strip off your clothes, plunge into the stream, allow the water to flow over you. After which you re-dress, take another drink, fill your canteen, note the time of the night —2:30—and with your canteen by your side lie down under a near-by fig-tree to spend some of the night in thought, the balance in sleep. This is contentment. This is life.

Was it by chance the dog barked? It was only one of a half-dozen small things that had happened during the last thirty hours. The missing of any one of them might have meant death.

Was it by chance, on the night previous, I met the prospectors?

Was it by chance the questionable water, with which I filled my canteen, was good?

Was it by chance, when I was struggling with the heat in Death Valley, a prayer was said for me?

Was it by chance, when I needed spurring on I had exceedingly dismal thoughts, thus causing me to have far more incentive ones than I otherwise would have had?

Was it by chance, although a mile away, at the opportune time a dog's bark was heard?

Was it by chance? I'll leave it to my readers to answer these questions.

AN OASIS IN DEATH VALLEY

Furnace Creek Ranch or "Borax" Smith's ranch lies in Death Valley on Furnace Creek.

It is a pretty spot there by itself—no other vegetation lying within fifty miles of it, no matter in which direction you might go. A goodly sized orchard is there containing a great number of fig-trees, and a large tract of grass and hay land lies beyond.

The stream that irrigates this land is a large one formed from springs at a few miles distant up the mountains—the Furnace Creek road as it goes out of the valley, following it to its source.

In Death Valley and adjacent to it are located the largest borax fields in the world. From these "Borax" Smith has made his millions. He has enough borax to supply the world and it is said he controls ninety percent of the entire borax fields and mines known of to-day, at any rate, it is conceded he has practically a corner on the American supply. It is also said he has holdings elsewhere in England and Russia.

His Death Valley supply of Borax is taken to the railroad with a twenty-mule team.

Before one arrives at Furnace Creek you pass the Old Borax Works about two miles above it. It is not being operated at present and is only operated during the most favorable part of the year. The main work now being done is near Daggett, but his main mine of all his numerous ones and the largest borax mine in the world is his "Lila

C."—which lies east of the Funeral Range and west of Eagle Mountain.

It is at this Furnace Creek Ranch that he keeps his stock, when not in use, and also raises hay for them when they are. A party by the name of Lentt—C. A. Lentt—is there in charge.

This is also where "Scotty" keeps a change of burros—there being three burros there of "Mysterious Scott's" at the time of my visit. Lentt thinks "Scotty" has a mine and one need not talk with him long before one can tell he is conscientious in his belief. He says—"Scotty is a good, congenial fellow. A fellow nice to meet. He pays his way and he comes and goes at haphazard. When he goes in you can see no ore but when he comes out he exhibits sacks of it." When I asked Lentt if he ever had hold of any of the stuff he said he had—and when I asked him if he ever panned any of it, he answered—"Pan it! You don't have to pan it. It is half gold." Continuing he said—"It is as much of a mystery to me where his mine is, as it is to any one else. We can see his camp fire in the mountains the next night after he leaves here but after that he is lost sight of, but up to the time he gets here on these trips into the mountains, his whereabouts is known. In talking he has often made the remark—'They hadn't better come up my canyon or I'll take a shot at them.'"

THROUGH THE LARGEST BORAX MINE

There are two kinds of borax—the Cotton-ball and the Colemanite—the first is more of a placer proposition, while the latter is in ledges the same as quartz mines.

While "Borax" Smith owns a great number of borax mines in Death Valley—his main property and the greatest borax mine in the world lies several miles off of Death Valley, to the east, in a mountain a few miles west of Eagle Mountain. It is known as the "Lila C." mine and it was the writer's privilege to be shown through this mine from start to finish.

This property lies, I should judge, about forty miles southeast of the Furnace Creek Ranch. The nearest habitation is an Indian family living up Ash Meadows and twenty-eight miles distant.

It is to this property that "Borax" Smith is building his railroad—from Ludlow, California, which lies on the main line of the Sante Fe, a great distance south.

The borax is Colemanite—being true fissure veins of borax. The numerous ledges being from six to twelve feet in width. The contacts are lime. There is over 1,200 lineal feet of ledge matter blocked out. There was also 5,000 tons on the dumps ready for shipment and as it is worth sixty dollars per ton in the mine there was one-third of a million dollars worth on the dumps and that is just taken out on development work.

It is said that "Borax" Smith will buy any borax property that amounts to anything that is discovered.

THE PIUTES IN SESSION—GRAND POW WOW

The week which ended Sunday, September 3rd, 1905, marked the commencement of a new epoch in the history of the Piute Tribe of Indians.

The entire week had been given over to a Grand Pow Wow in which Indian dancing, athletic performances, which showed fleetness and strength of limb, and games of chance, galore, were on tap.

A few speeches were made—by the wise ones—same as white man.

This event, which was given at Pahrump, was a religious one in honor of their late great chief—and peacemaker—Tacopa, who has within the past year, at a very ripe old age, passed over to the Happy Hunting Grounds. It was in honor of him and to elect a new chief for the tribe.

The Monte Cristo of Death Valley 123

The Piutes came from all around—from any direction you might wave your hand. There were big braves, younger ones, the squaws and Indian lassies there in great numbers. They were there to the extent of three to four hundred strong from all parts.

There were Tacopa John and Tacopa Charley—young braves of the good old chief and peacemaker, who is now in the Happy Hunting Grounds. Tacopa John, who is the oldest offspring of the ex-chief was made the new chief of the Piutes.

Then there was Panamint Tom, captain over all the Piutes that call the whole of the Panamint Range—across Death Valley, their home—with some of his followers there.

There was Captain Kearney of the Timber Mountains and followers. It was near Captain Kearney's Mountains, at Pahrump, that the Pow Wow was held. Then there was Ash Meadow Charley, captain, and followers from the Funeral Range beside the great celebrities—Doctor Umber Seat, or the Chief Medicine Man of all the tribe; Indian Chief Johnson who is known extensively and whose territory is all that from beyond the Mohave on the west, to Needles on the east, also "Big Mary," or Sitia, the Chief Gambler—who kept good her previous record by winning all the big money. She and others came from where the Colorado flows—the Grand Canyon—over a hundred and twenty miles distant.

Many others were there from all parts—in fact they were all there—the followers of the big chief.

On the last night of the big Pow Wow they burnt up $400.00 worth of blankets—among them some Navajo blankets that would cost as much as $25.00 per pair, and dress goods, made-up, and other articles, also killed seven head of horses. These things were all sent to the departed chief and his squaws for their use in the other world.

In giving the history of the departed chief it is best told in Captain Kearney's own words. Captain Kearney of the Timber Mountains was born and raised in Nye Country. He is a full-blooded Indian but speaks plain English words—but sentences disconnected. He is modest about himself but full of praise for other people.

"Chief Tacopa—big warrior—kill white man," as he gave his hand a southerly swing—"Stump Springs, Resting Springs, Mountain Springs, Las Vegas—all over. Big Warrior. Long time—sixty years ago—made peace. Long talk—long three-day talk—John Morris—long hair—shoulders—like cowboy—still alive—round here now. Long talk—three days. Stump Springs. Shook hands—John Morris—good friends. Chief came back—Said 'Last time—no more kill. No more kill white man—white man no more kill Indian. White man Indian friend.'"

SCOTTY'S "CAMP HOLD OUT" FOUND

While the summer has been hot for prospecting, especially in the Funeral Range on the side that hugs Death Valley—there have been very few diligently prospecting there, but as it is a large scope of territory the mountains are practically unseen yet, to say nothing of being prospected.

Most of those who have been there have been able to stake off some good prospects that show good surface showings, but as yet no one has found "Scotty's" mine. There is no denying the fact they have all kept an "eagle eye" open to find it, or they would have been prospecting some of the other numerous ranges in Nevada that are not in as close proximity to Death Valley and are also as rich in mineral resources.

One thing has been accomplished though during the summer. "Scotty's" camp, and more than probable, his main one, has been discovered. It is located off the southern part of Death Valley and to the east, in a high mountain known as Mount Smith—up a very steep, and

THE MONTE CRISTO OF DEATH VALLEY 125

in places, almost inaccessible canyon—which goes up from the Death Valley side.

Among the first that went there claim it is in places so precipitous that ropes were necessary to accomplish the climb and in other places what little inlet there was up the canyon was clogged up with large boulders that had been placed there and which had to be removed before they could proceed further on their way. In other places, lower down in the canyon, where burros could travel but where they had to climb up a slanting place over a solid rock foundation, allowing them no foothold, it would be impossible for a horse to make it.

Since the discovery of this camp of "Mysterious Scott's," or "Death Valley Scott," etc., there have been a score or more, prospectors and others, who have made it, and their stories all confirm each other. Among the visitors—but not among the original discoverers—were our friends, Miles and Brown, previously mentioned in this book. Among others were two more prospectors—Herman Kah and Mike Jordan. They had been there as recently as September 5th and it was the writer's pleasure to meet them just a day or two later and he got the following facts about the camp directly from them.

It is located in Mount Smith, quite a number of miles up the fourth canyon from the north, that leads out of Death Valley, into the mountain. While none of these canyons have a stream either at the head or foot of the canyon—all four have a stream up the canyon a ways. At the time of their visit, so many had gone ahead that there was quite a path leading up and it was quite easy of access from the Death Valley side. But it was a total impossibility for any one to get to it from the upper end of the range as there were numerous high cliffs—straight up and down—any one of which would be impossible to make.

The camp itself is a hole in the solid rock; another large rock overhangs forming the other sides. These overhanging rocks almost come together at the top, there being an opening above of only a few feet.

"Scotty" has named the camp—"Camp Hold Out," there being a placard to that effect. It is supposed to be "Scotty's" main camp, as it is equipped with pieces of furniture that are to be found only in a few homes in the cities in the New Goldfields of Nevada. For instance— he has a bath-tub and a large easy rocker. As the bath-tub is full length and the chair heavy, these prospectors say he must be a good "lugger" to have ever conveyed these things up there.

His provisions and canned goods are of the very best brands and he has a large assortment of them that the most fastidious of persons could not complain of even if they wanted to. Among them he has many nicknacks such as, after-dinner mints, etc.

"Scotty" holds "open house" here, the same as at the "Great Northern" or any place else he happens to be, and it looks as though he has this camp as much for the convenience of the prospector who might happen along, while he is out in the world—Los Angeles, Chicago, New York, San Francisco, and other places enjoying himself, as much as for anything else—as the following notice is conspicuously placed:—

"Whenever you come here, eat all you want, stay as long as you want, but don't take nothing away.
Walter Scott."

Also another notice which reads:—

"Look out for the pet rattle-snake. Don't kill her. She won't bite you. Walter Scott."

The walls were literally covered with pictures and one thing and another. These pictures consisted mainly of famous actors and actresses, Buffalo Bill's Wild West people and prominent men. Among other things posted on the wall was a letter of introduction, from the Deputy Sheriff of Los Angeles County to the Sheriff of San Bernardino County, stating that he was a Rough Rider, man of integrity, etc. These wall decorations were so numerous that these prospectors say it took fully an hour to look them over.

Another thing that made the boys laugh was a large array of solid silver spoons that he had as souvenirs. They were laid side by side. There was one from each of the leading railroads and hotels in the country—The Southern Pacific, Sante Fe, Salt Lake, Erie, Burlington and many more of the railroads were represented, besides a great many of the leading hotels throughout the country—one from each of them.

Directly above "Scotty's" camp—up the canyon—is quite a flow of water—considerably more than "Scotty" has. This is filed upon by a Cherokee half-breed Indian—Billy Kee. These locations are in Inyo County, California.

While "Scotty's" camp, and it looks to be his main one—has been discovered, his mine is not located there. These two prospectors made several pannings for placer even, on the ground, but were unable to raise a "color." Others have covered the entire territory, for a radius of three miles, but have been unable to discover any workings whatever. While men have been diligent, the location of his mine is as much of a mystery to-day as it ever was.

APACHE INDIAN AND DEATH VALLEY MINER BANKER GIRARD AFTER AN ACCOUNTING

The newspapers which came into camp about September 12th under heading "Los Angeles, September 7th," stated that Banker Julian N. Girard of New York had one of his agents at that city (Los Angeles), to get an accounting from "Scotty." This agent was Antonio Apache—a full-blooded Indian, but a college graduate.

The "Los Angeles Examiner" interviewed both parties and the following facts, greatly reduced, were taken from that paper.

"Scotty," after getting a letter at Barstow from Mr. Apache and also getting a telegram from Mr. Girard, finally met the agent at the "Lankershim Hotel"—Los Angeles—and from all reports he talked pretty plainly to the agent—as he thought the agent was responsible for some rot written about him (Scotty) in one of the leading Chicago papers. The agent, and also Mr. Girard's telegram, told "Scotty," he (the agent) was there in the interest of Mr. Girard to see that the claims were properly recorded and to look out for his interests in general and also to be shown the property, as he has never received any remuneration from the mine that had been found through his "grub stake" and that it was about time to be shown the goods.

"Scotty" says that Girard has no interest in the property. He admits that Girard "grub staked" him a few years ago but that he considers Girard—and has for a long time back—to be down and out. He says he found a mine in the Death Valley region but it looked to be low grade, although he had found some high grade values, but he thought they were kidneys at that time. He thought though they could make a mine out of it if he had the chance to work it and went to New York and put it to Mr. Girard to that effect. But Mr. Girard said that Death Valley did not look good to him. Afterwards when he ("Scotty") kept appealing to Girard to work the mine as he had found some high-grade stuff, Girard repeatedly informed him that a Death Valley proposition did not look good enough for him to put any money in working it and to put it in this bronco buster's own words—"He threw me and threw me high into the air. I at one time sent him twenty dollars worth of telegrams but he ignored them all and at a time when I needed his help the most. Afterwards he 'laid down' altogether."

"Scotty" says he is ready to repay him, dollar for dollar, every cent that Mr. Girard at one time advanced him, which amounted to about $4,000 in all, but otherwise he would do nothing as he had for a long time back considered him down and out.

Antonio Apache says,-as he understands it,—Mr Girard had on several occasions tried to get "Scotty" to show parties the property to examine it but "Scotty" always had some excuse.

Mr. Apache has communicated with Mr. Girard the result of the conversation and says it is up to him now what course to pursue.

"MYSTERIOUS SCOTT."

After being out all summer—"Mysterious Scott" went back into Death Valley and Funeral Range presumably to his "Camp Hold Out."

He outfitted at Barstow, having eight burros, and went in the latter part of September. He also got his burros at Furnace Creek Ranch, although the feed bill for the summer, besides the trouble of getting them, was far more than the burros were worth.

He was in the mountains three weeks on this trip staying several days longer than he anticipated. He had a rough journey of it coming out. He arrived at Barstow about sunrise having traveled all night as well as, at least, the previous night. He spent the day in sleep, having for his pillow sacks of ore. He also held a grip on his rifle which lay over him.

A TRIBUTE TO THE BURRO

The much abused burro finds its place in the mining world of Nevada. There is many a mine that has been discovered during the last two years and a far greater number more will be found during the next few years, that if it wasn't for this little sure-footed pack-animal, which has been shipped into the state in large numbers, would for years to come be undiscovered.

The burro is the prospectors' friend. It gives the man of moderate means a chance to look for the vast riches of this part of the country which is as a rule devoid of grazing. A burro hustles for itself and thrives on the growth here where a horse, or even a mule, would starve to death. Hay, at the present time, in the Bullfrog District where there is a population of three thousand people and where freighting is made a business of, is $5.00 per hundred pounds, or $100.00 per ton; barley is 6c per pound. This is with the railroad facilities far nearer and better than a few months previous. So one can see how this little animal has won laurels here, with prospectors that haven't more than thirty dollars a month to prospect on. The burro requires a little barley the days used, but otherwise it hustles for itself.

There are other features that commend the burros for universal use to prospectors here besides the feed feature.

They can stand far more grief than either horse or mule by doing without water longer. Also they have an instinct to find water. The prospectors who have been saved from dying of thirst in a territory unknown to them, through his burro ferreting out a spring, possibly miles away, have not been few.

A good prospector will never get out of water—but I have heard one say if he ever did lose water he would stick to his burro if he had to tie himself on it. It might take the burro some time but he will eventually, invariably, get to water.

A SUNSET

A pleasant sight to look upon is a sunset in Rhyolite. The mountains to the west and north do not get the sun's fair rays. Those to the south in the Funeral Range across the valley that lead towards Las Vegas—get the sun diagonally of the range so to speak—that together with the hot blue air from Death Valley, beyond, causes it to have a dark blue hue, while the mountains to the east and across the Amargosa get the benefit of it full in the face, giving them a reddish tinge.

The scene does not last long though—but gradually moves away, leaving the observer in thoughtful meditation about the grandeur of this world.

AN AFTERNOON SHOWER

There lies behind the village of Beatty, on the Amargosa River, a mountain with strata of many hues—there are light brown, dark brown, pink, yellow, green, then the dark brown again.

A passing afternoon shower washes this rainbow-tinted mountain. The fleeting clouds soon go and the sun comes out and kisses the newly washed mountain making it even more brilliant than before.

Below this mountain and to the northward is the valley of the Amargosa—it in turn is greener than before, while in the sky, above this kissed, blushing mountain, can be seen a real rainbow—crowning it all.

LIFE IN THE MOUNTAINS

There is something about life in the mountains that is elevating. One has only to look at the hills and the peaks and the blue sky above to grasp some idea of life.

They even appeal to an everyday man far more than do the stars. These hills and peaks are always with us—a part of us—and not at some inconceivable distance. While with us they are still the work of another hand.

I can see how it is possible for one in a contaminated and congested city, where he sees so much work of man—to lose track of the greater power that is behind all, but put that same man out here where he has a chance of being "alone with his own conscience," as my friend Gene Mayfield would put it, with mountains on all sides—Would it be possible for there to be one who would think there is no other power besides himself, you and I?

True, we do not have churches here as soon as in other communities, but better still, we always have these hills and peaks to help us have healthier and nobler thoughts and also a better chance of doing some thinking for ourselves.

A WORD TO PROSPECTORS

Good prospectors, those who have found things, say—Many a prospector makes a mistake by taking in too much territory and not getting out of the new, but beaten trails. For instance—they are at Searchlight, then they get it into their heads to go to the Funeral Range or to Lida or over to Kawich, thus keeping on the beaten trail and practically just make from water to water. A great many such globe trotters find themselves out of provisions and finally out of money with which to buy more, with practically no territory prospected, then they have to either get a "grub stake" or stop and work awhile so as to earn enough for another start.

There is good prospecting territory, and will be for a great number of years, in all parts of the extensive mineral belt of Nevada and the prospector who goes at it in a systematic manner, using diligence and more or less thoroughness about his work, will stand a very good chance of finding something.

To thoroughly prospect a mountain, to use it in its broadest sense, before leaving it, is practically impossible, as that takes a long time, but for a prospector when he gets into "likely" looking mountains—to stay with them awhile is not a bad idea.

A prospector wishing to prospect a group of mountains should have his base of supplies where there is water—then take as long prospecting tours out from there as he wishes to and get out of the beaten trails. But he should always know where there is water and he should always keep within range of it and better still always have some on hand. While prospecting the hills he will more than probably find other water and can then change his camp if he so desires.

Besides his outfit; pick and shovel, piston, mortar and pans, cooking utensils, provisions, bedding, etc., and always water, there are a few nicknacks a prospector should never be without—Among them are compass, jack-knife, matches, and magnifying glass, especially the first three and more especially the compass. A watch does not come in badly as that with the sun is a check on your compass and your compass, together with the sun, is in turn a check on your watch. So together with the sun, one is the check on the work of the other and vice versa.

Nevada is a good state to prospect in during the Fall, Winter and Spring, as the winters are said to be mild. One cannot prospect to an advantage during the heated summer months—while the nights are always cool and it is also always comfortable in the shade, it is too hot to prospect to advantage in the sun's rays. If a person really does prospect during July and August it is not a bad idea to get up as early as two o'clock if necessary, have breakfast, put a slap-jack in your pocket, and get where you wish to prospect by daylight, then do your prospecting for a few hours and "knock off" at noon or early in the afternoon for the day, but there are very few who prospect much during these two months.

"CHUCKAWALLA MIKE'S" STORIES

It was an evening in midsummer. A bunch of us were seated in front of one of the principal restaurants, and watering resorts, in the camp, enjoying the climate when a recent arrival from the east joined the crowd. He carried under his arm a new pair of boots and stated to one of the party he was going to have them "pegged."

Here "Chuckawalla Mike"—an old time prospector—spoke up and said—"That reminds me of an experience I once had. I was on one of my prospecting trips one day with a bunch of three burros when, lo and behold, two of them stopped dead still on me. I could not get them to move a step. Not knowing what was up I gave them all the cuss names I knew of—more than I ever gave them before and that is saying a mighty lot. All they would do was to flap ears, switch their tails, and look content. I decided, then and there, to enter them into the slow burro race which was going to be pulled off the Fourth. Regardless of that consolation I became mighty riled and started around them so as to whip them over their noses, as I saw whipping them from behind had no effect. I had not made but a few steps, starting to go around them, as I was, when something seemed to grab the bottom of my boot causing it to come down on the ground faster than usual. I made another step, with the other foot when the same thing happened to it. The earth seemed to come up to meet the foot and the foot to go down to meet the earth—and there I stuck. I could not budge one or the other. I could swing my body backward and forward but I could not navigate. As I exerted myself the sweat soon came out on me in beads and I was almost fagged out. I attempted to lie down and rest a spell, but one foot being in front of the other a pace, I could not even do that. Well, to make a long story short, I finally managed to extricate myself from my boots and after taking a rest, I inaugurated an investigation.

"I found that the burros and myself had stepped on a ledge of magnetic iron. The ledge was some twenty feet in width. The burros—the two that got stuck being shod—of course were magnetized to the ledge and when I stepped on the ledge—having nails in the bottom of my boots—before and aft—I was also magnetized to the ledge. As I could do nothing for the burros and they looked so contented, I in my stocking feet, got on the third one—which had never been shod—and we wended our way to camp.

"The burros are still there and can be seen any day as contented as you please—magnetized to the ledge, as is also my pair of high-topped boots,—but no Chuckawalla Mike in them to tell the story. He would sooner tell the story over a camp fire."

"Yes, while that is one of my most exasperating experiences, I have had others—more narrow escapes where my life was in more danger.

"One day—when I was conducting my profession, prospecting these hills—I got away from water and got lost. I don't know exactly how many days and nights I was without water for I forgot to keep on calculating them, but there came the time when I was pert near all in—when I thought for sure I would have to bid good-bye to these old hills—in fact, I had given up entirely when I saw a man standing up in front of me. He was a good six-footer and I saw he was dead—but he was standing up with his right arm raised and outstretched, pointing his forefinger in a southerly direction, towards a hill. I took a survey of the hill he was pointing to, which was several rods distance, and lo and behold there was a large green spot. I knew what it meant—there, there was water. The thoughts of it made me feel as frisky as a two-year old colt in a clover-patch—and it was only a minute before I was there, finding one of the nicest springs you ever gazed on."

Jim, another prospector, who had experienced being without water for a few hours one day, and those few hours had caused him to commence to realize what it meant to be without water on the desert, interrupted Mike by repeating the saying—"A camel can go eight days without a drink, but who wants to be a camel" and stepping to the door gave the order—"Bartender! give the crowd a drink and be sure and remember Mike."

After the round of drinks—Mike, taking whiskey and pouring himself out a goodly sized one, got started on another story.

"Another time when I was intending to cross Death Valley—there seemed to be something telling me not to go. I had made Funeral Range and was down on the Death Valley side. That something seemed to keep on telling me more strongly than ever, but, I was not turning back and was about to start across when I ran into a prospector with a bunch of burros. They were all dead—this prospector and his burros. The burros were standing up—dead—eating greasewood bushes and the prospector was standing up—dead—shaking his head from one side to the other. Maybe you think I didn't take the nudge and not attempt to make the trip."

The tenderfoot who had been taking in the stories said to a bystander—"I don't believe that." "Chuckawalla Mike," who overheard the remark, turned around and addressing the new arrival from the east said in a matter-of-fact way—"While I saw it with my own eyes, sometimes I hardly believe it myself."

SCOTTY'S PROBABLE DEATH

C. D. Brown—who has been prospecting continually in the Funeral Range and Death Valley country this fall as well as the summer months—came from the lower part of Death Valley into camp—Rhyolite—December 13th, with sad news of Scotty's probable death.

This Man-of-the-Mines of Death Valley, together with his brother who has been accompanying him a part of the way of late, on these perilous trips, but not the entire distance, got into Salt Wells, which lies in Death Valley a few miles south of Bennett Wells, two weeks prior. The two Scotts put up there for the night.

Scotty told a bunch of prospectors there of being followed and if the fellow still persisted in keeping it up, he said he would fix him. The next morning "Mysterious Scott" and his riding mule were gone. His brother, with the pack-train, proceeded to Bennett Wells only a few miles distant. Scotty has not been heard or seen since. But several days afterwards his riding mule came into Salt Wells—riderless. The mule had no bridle but had a saddle on. A bullet of some large caliber had pierced the cantle of the saddle. Large clots of blood were on a blanket attached to saddle and the mule also carried a bullet in its haunch.

At first they had not thought very much of Scotty's disappearance, as they presumed he had struck out alone, during the middle of the night, only to "side step" the people that were known to have been endeavoring to follow him on these trips for some month's past and also so he could make to the place where his hidden treasure was located, alone. But when the mule came back, riderless, showing conclusively there had been a fierce battle in which the rider had been pierced by a bullet, there was much speculation as to the outcome.

Scotty's brother was notified at Bennett Wells and he and a friend by the name of Frazier immediately struck out to hunt for Scotty. They started for Wind Gate Pass, which is in the lower part of Death Valley and of all the inaccessible parts of Death Valley that vicinity was considered the worst. Frazier came back after a few hours out, but as Scotty's brother hadn't returned when Brown left, no other news was to be had—but everything looked bad.

"Mysterious Scott" is known to be a crack shot, in fact there are very few, if any, on the plains and in the mountains that are better. His being right at home in all the more rugged parts of the country has given him a good eye for distance, which is a large handicap over the ordinary man in this unknown country of many diversified elevations.

With his keen eye, quick action and steady nerve, while it is evident that Scotty is hit—it is thought that he in turn has two or three to his credit.

Those who know him best, think that he must have been shot at from ambush. Not because there cannot be two at any shooting affray, but "Mysterious Scott" was always so well prepared with field-glasses, long-ranged rifles, etc. that they could not see how any one could get the bead on him out in the open. He also takes such precautions, especially can this be said since the country has commenced to be prospected.

Brown said that neither one of Scotty's rifles were in the leather cases, that hung on the saddle when the mule came in, both of them being empty. We felt as though this was a good indication that Scotty was still alive. The large clots of blood on the saddle and blanket showed he was not unseated immediately. The rifles being gone, unless confiscated by the enemy, in which event they would have been apt to have killed or taken the mule, indicated he was still alive and was more than probably barricading himself against them. Possibly he was dying by slow degrees from his wound or was wounded and dying of hunger and sent his mule out for aid. Again he might have been able to ride his mule to one of his numerous caches, or possibly to his mine, wherever it is, but felt he could not continue.

Many were the opinions expressed by the boys in the camp that evening and many a head was shaken with the remark—"Too bad, too bad," and many were the remarks such as, "I hope he'll come out all right,"or similar ones, uttered. Why? Because Scotty is a whole-souled fellow. And we all honor him because he keeps the best of us guessing as to the source of his fabulous wealth. While it looked bad, in our inner hearts, many of us, as we went to our tents and our cots that evening, had confidence in him—That if any one was equal to the occasion, he would be.

During the course of the next few days, the newspapers that came into the camp from the outside world—four days old—stated that Scotty was being followed to his gold mine when seen last.

One article was under heading of "Los Angeles" and was practically as follows:—

S. M. Mangus, who has been prospecting, together with a partner, in the Death Valley country for some time, saw Scotty near Bennett Wells. Mr. Mangus was coming on the outside for more provisions when he met Scotty going in towards what is known as Scotty's country. Scotty had not made Bennett Wells yet and was alone riding his favorite mule, when seen by Mangus. He was on scout duty, being some distance ahead of his pack outfit at the time, taking in the country pretty generally as he advanced. Scotty had with him two field-glasses, one for night service as well as one for day, two long-ranged rifles, also a brace of six-shooters.

Scotty told Mangus that he had been followed for

some distance—by whom he did not say—but that the party saw to it that he did not give him (Scotty) a chance for a good shot. Scotty also said he expected to be out again by New Years if everything went well.

Mangus met Scotty's brother with a four-burro outfit bringing up the rear some three miles behind.

Another article which came a couple of days later stated that William Lawton, another Death Valley prospector who got on the outside about the middle of December, reports having met Scotty and his brother camping near Bennett Wells at the time of Scotty's disappearance, some two weeks past. Walter Scott told him that they (the Scotts) had been trailed for some time past by a man riding a "Red Mule," but that they had failed to get into communication with the party. Several times they would stop but the man would stop also. When they would prolong their stop the man would prolong his; when they would move on again the man would follow; always keeping under cover, more or less, and at a safe distance. Scotty said he could wear him out waiting but he had no time to kill and that he didn't like this game of tag without a tag.

Before Lawton left camp, Scotty was gone. He went during a night. His brother, Bill, stated he went back under cover of night to find the man who was trailing him to get an explanation. Lawton came out of Death Valley by the way of the Wind Gate Pass. The Pass is a couple of days, journey from Bennett Wells, but met no one.

(This man on the "Red Mule" is supposed to be the same one who is known to have attempted, with others, to follow Scott into the country where his mine is located, in September.)

$1000 REWARD

Day after day passes on and nothing new is heard of Scotty. Highly paid scouts have been sent out from this district also from Barstow. $1000 reward is offered for his whereabouts. These scouts are scouring the country thoroughly. They have these following facts to work upon:—

Walter Scott left his camp near Bennett Wells in Death Valley Dec. 1.

His mule "Slim" galloped into camp Dec. 7, at 11:30 A. M.

The saddle cantle was pierced by a rifle ball and the saddle seat and blankets were blood-stained. Another bullet had entered the mule's haunch.

Up to Dec. 10, Bill Scott and his scouts had not found any trace of the missing miner.

He was equipped with two rifles, field glasses and is supposed to have had $1800 on his person.

It is not thought he took any provisions with him other than water.

Many men have gone out in the endeavor to find him. Not only for the reward, as a great number had joined the search before that was offered, but also in hopes of locating his mine which is still a mystery as to its whereabouts. While Scotty has a great many friends, a great number of them that are taking up the hunt are not particularly interested in Scotty or in bringing his slayer to punishment and they know they can not all get the reward. But they are in hopes it will lead to the discovery of his fabulously rich gold mine, in which event there will be a general scramble to find other values in that vicinity.

The country in which Scotty is lost, or rather the country in which he left his brother and numerous other prospectors and is more than probably "winged" or is dead in—is over 150 miles from railroad. It is one of the most hazardous sections known of. While the camp where he left his brother is only 75 miles from the Bullfrog District, there are two almost unsurmountable obstacles—Funeral Range and Death Valley—between.

While there are numerous prospectors working the country, it is only known thoroughly by Scott and Indians. His knowing every Indian trail and hole in this region, where the high peaks frown on Death Valley below, is considered a big advantage he has over the ordinary man. He also has a sage-brush constitution to see him through ordeals that would kill nine out of ten of the regular run. What desert tragedy was enacted there in a fair fight no doubt Scotty had the odds in his favor. As there was a friendly feeling between him and all the Indians there is no doubt but that his enemies are, or "were"—is more than probably the right word to use,—white men. What the result was no doubt time will tell.

One of Scotty's closest friends, Rol King of Los Angeles, received word from Scotty's brother after a search in which he succeeded in following Scotty's mule tracks back covering a distance of over fifty miles through some of the roughest country on the face of the map. He had with him Shands Merrick, who has the reputation of being one of the most fearless and experienced scouts that ever tightened a girt in modern times. A "Death Valley" sand storm had blown up and had almost obliterated all marks that might otherwise have led to Scotty's whereabouts.

Following extracts were taken from "Bill" Scott's letter, written December 10. The letter was sent by courier to Post Office:—

"Scotty's mule 'Slim' came to my camp at Bennett's Wells on the 7th inst. at 11:30 a. m. with a bullet hole through the cantle of the saddle and considerable blood on the cantle, the seat and two big blotches of blood on the blanket, also bullet through 'Slim's' haunch.

"I at once took the mule's back track with Shand Merricks, who is a good scout. We camped two nights and a day on her trail. We tracked her over fifty miles over the roughest country.

"She came from the south end of Death Valley out of the Funeral Mountains.

"As there has been a terrible sandstorm raging for the last thirty-six hours it is almost impossible to do any trailing on account of the sand filling the mule's tracks.

"We got out of water and had to come in.

"Merricks has a good trailer with him and has gone back to where we lost 'Slim's' tracks.

"Scotty left me on the morning of December 1.

"He carried two rifles, a pair of field-glasses and $1800."

"Long Hank" who was in Rhyolite, from the south, for a half day Christmas, practically verified the above. He said the sand storm was still raging in Death Valley when he left but that it had been two weeks since he had been in the valley proper. He said while Merrick and Bill Scott were supposed to be on the main lead, that it was no "lead pipe cinch" that they were. As he understood it the trail was dim enough at its best. Every prospector in the country had joined the hunt and they all had their own notions as to territory and direction to go. Every sign that looked as though it might lead to something was being run down.

The great number of prospectors who had wanted to follow Scott for the last two years, but would not because they were friends of his or were afraid to do so, now felt as though the field was open. Especially since the reward was offered. Also those who were known to have attempted to follow him on various occasions on his treasure-getting trips into this region, but had been "side-stepped" one way or another, were enthusiastic in their search. Almost every prospector within a radius of 150 miles was looking for Scotty and his mine and many a point around a rock would be searched that had never had man within miles of it before.

"Long Hank" had been confining his search after leaving Death Valley to the Funeral Range. He says on his return he is going to work further east where the country is more open. That there might be the mere possibility that Scotty's mine is the old lost Breyfogle mine, in which event it is more apt to be somewhere between Ash Meadows and Stump Springs, which lies below White's (Manse). But that it is generally supposed by practically all the boys that it is located in some of the rougher parts nearer Death Valley as Death Valley is the last region that Scotty is seen in on these mysterious trips, where he gets his limitless supply of gold.

SCOTTY NOT IN "CAMP HOLD OUT"

The following was taken from the Los Angeles Examiner—under date Dec. 23

The fate of Scotty remains a mystery. Rol King was kept busy all day yesterday answering personal inquiries and telephone calls for information, but to all the same reply was made, "We have nothing authentic."

E. F. Cain of 535 Wall street returned to Los Angeles yesterday with the statement that he had been staying at Walter Scott's camp, and sleeping in his bunk, from December 10 to 16. He says that he saw nothing of the missing Death Valley miner, and left too early to meet the scouts that are out searching for him.

The camp he refers to is situated, he says, a few miles above the mouth of what is generally known as Scott's canyon, in the southerly end of the Funeral Range of mountains, about twenty miles south of Bennett's Wells.

He says that as he approached the camp he recognized the tracks of Scotty's mule, Slim, and that they did not enter the canyon, but just approached the mouth of it. He says he did not observe which way they turned, not having heard of the incident of the mule's having returned to Bennett's Wells riderless at that time. Mr. Cain said last night:

"I did not know that Scotty was missing until I returned to Los Angeles. I was at his camp in Scott's canyon from December 10 to 16 and saw nothing of him.

"The camp was unoccupied, and I used it during my entire stay, sleeping on his mattress.

"My partner accompanied me. We saw only two men while we were there. One Bill Kees, or better known as the "Wild Man." The other was a prospector, who informed us that he had passed Bill Scott and the burros at Rhoad's Wells, near by, but had seen nothing of Walter.

"No scout or search party came near us while we were there.

"As we made our way to the camp we plainly recognized Scotty's trail, both from the hoof-prints of Slim and an empty whisky flask of a brand such as no one else but Scotty has in that part of the country.

"The tracks were fresh. He must have been only a day ahead of us. I do not remember seeing the trail enter the canyon. I did not know of his disappearance, either when I went there or when I left, and so paid no attention to which way they turned.

"So far as is known, Scotty has only unworked mining claims in the vicinity of this camp. He once told my partner—that he had a mine thirty miles distant. I do not know in which direction he meant.

"He told my partner the water was so scarce there that he could only work the mine by himself, and for a few days at a time.

"His camp, at which we stayed, is built under an overhanging shelf of rock, and right at the best water hole in the canyon. He has it fixed up very comfortably.

"Kees showed us a piece of white quartz in which we could discern gold at a distance of seven feet. He said that he had obtained it upon one of Scotty's claims.

A party from Salt Wells reports that Scotty's brother has returned to that point from another several days' search in the mountains, and reported he had found his brother and that he was "unhurt." What happened on the desert in Death Valley or in that rugged mountainous country, that is known thoroughly only by Scott, which hems Death Valley on all sides—is still a mystery.

Scotty's brother's explanation of several things are not very clear, says this "desert rat."

This brother accounts for the clots of blood as coming from a mountain sheep, which his brother had "potted" as he puts it, and the accidental discharge of his gun as he (Scotty) was placing the sheep on the saddle accounts for bullet hole. This "desert rat" says while that might be possible there are two bullet holes to account for and many other things. He believes Scotty is safe all right or they would not give up the hunt but believes there are liable to be three or four bodies run across that were not victims of Death Valley heat this past summer.

This "desert rat" thought even if the worst did happen in this unknown country that Scotty did the right thing as it is considered very bad form to follow one in this western country. He says there are several things that Scotty's brother cannot explain satisfactorily to the boys. And they are asking themselves these questions—If Bill Scott was not telling the truth, and they had their own opinion about it, why wasn't he? Was Scotty the aggressor? And what has become of the man on the "Red Mule?" These are questions they asked themselves and immediately satisfied themselves in their own minds.

TWO DESERT BATTLES

After being out for almost six weeks and during the major portion of that time over one hundred men were scouring the country for him Scotty reaches Barstow, Jan. 2. He has bullet through leg. He received his bullet in fight with outlaws as he with two others—a white and an Indian —were coming out of the rough country near Wind Gate Pass as late as Dec. 31. Scotty and his party were caught off guard and were attacked by three men there in a three-cornered fight.

He also admits having another fight on Dec. 5. He was uninjured then but his Shoshone Indian, who was riding mule at the time, was slightly wounded. After his last fight on the desert, he, with a 30–30 steel jacketed bullet wound through his leg, rides 133 miles to Barstow within 33 hours. Upon reaching there he is so weak and exhausted that he has to be helped from saddle and is put to bed.

The last battle happened while they were riding through a rough gulch, and as he had come out from that inaccessible lost country where his mine is supposed to be located, he had thrown aside some of his precautions. The path was a rocky one, and there was a storm of sleet driving into the faces of the travelers.

It was a time when living things seemed to have abandoned the arid waste and Scotty, with all his shrewdness, would not have believed there was a man within the range of vision.

WAITED ON TRAIL FOR SCOTT

"The men were awaiting on the trail for us," explained Scotty. "There were three of them, and they were hid behind the rocks. It was a kind of three-cornered canyon where they caught us.

"They didn't give me much show. They had me clear down before I knew they were around. The two men with me were all right. I knew I could trust them. We figured that our guns were just as good as theirs and that we had them any way they played."

Scotty says he knows the men who attempted to kill him. His explanation of the attack is that the men thought he was returning from his mine and that by killing him, they could get his location papers or in lieu of them, get some valuable data that would give them some inkling to where his mine is located.

"Those fellows thought they had the location of the ground down pretty fine," said Scotty, "but they knew it was hopeless to look without the papers. That is why they wanted to get me and it meant, dead, for that is the only way they could take them."

SCOTTY'S EARLIER FIGHT

But little can be learned from Scott of his earlier fight. He says another man was riding the mule which came into camp riderless the next day. His companion at that time, he says, was but slightly wounded by the bullet which struck the saddle. The mule was frightened, had got a bullet herself, and ran away, carrying the evidences of the conflict back to camp. Having escaped so easily himself, Scotty did not think much about the alarm that would be occasioned by the appearance of the mule. He was interested in the theories that had been advanced to account for his supposed plight. As to the mystery of the disappearance of the guns, which are usually strapped to his burro, Scotty says they were removed when the other man rode him and that was why he came into camp with nothing but the saddle showing the bullet hole and blood stains.

Scotty has always anticipated trouble in his visits to the desert and he generally takes every precaution possible, but he had got out so far on his way home that he had become careless.

SCOTTY RELATES STORY

The next day after Scotty reached Barstow he takes the train to Los Angeles and as it pulled into the station, numerous friends got on board to welcome Scotty home and lend him any assistance they might. As they proceeded to the lounge on which he lay, a smile came over his otherwise haggard face.

"I'm bent up a bit," he said with a grin, "but I'll call the turn on all of them yet. Hospital? Not for me. I want a bed. You fellows don't know what a bed means to a man who has been weeks out on the desert fighting for his life and his fortune."

Friends lifted the desert mystery up and stuck his crutches under his arms. Then came slow progress to the car platform.

"Scotty," said one of them, "there are some photographers waiting with a flashlight to take your picture—don't you jump when the thing goes off."

"Jump!" said Scotty, with a snort. "I may jump a bit when rifles are popping about, but don't fear that I'll duck at a flashlight," and he did not. The depot master got him a wheel chair, which rolled him out to the street.

He was loaded into the motor car and driven up to the

Hollenbeck, where he was given a picon punch, and then taken to his rooms.

These are up two flights of stairs, and he insisted on hobbling up with a hop and a one-leg sort of step, disdaining all aid until his door was reached, and then, though the heart was brave the muscles and nerves petered out, and he sank on his bed with quivering features, though without a groan.

In a few seconds he was himself again.

"The story?" he said. "Why it is not much. We had two scraps, and things were lively for a time, but I played them, and here I am.

"The first fight was on December 5, in the valley. They winged poor old Jack, my Shoshone Indian—got him in the hip—but he's all right; he'll get well. Jack was riding my mule 'Slim' that time, and when the bullet struck him he fell. Just before that they had sniped 'Slim'—put a bullet through his haunch—and 'Slim' objected. He rared in the air, which threw Jack for'ard, and saved his life, for the bullet they sent at him went through the cantle and struck him in the thigh, making a flesh wound, but nothing bad. Jack fell, and the mule went on to the camp.

"You see I did not have any fear up to then, for I knew it would do them no good to kill me until after I had my claims all right.

"Jack"—this was to his wife—"open that grip and show the boys those records."

Mrs. Scott opened the sack and pulled out a lot of legal documents. Scott handled them lovingly.

"Those are the titles to my claims. There are sixteen of them, and some of them are 'Darbys.' After I got those I knew I might have trouble. And it came.

"We were just this side of Wind Gate Pass when we had the second go, on Sunday, December 31. That is in the open. Not much cover. Jackson, my old desert man, was riding ahead, when z-z-zip, I heard a bullet sing by him; then another and another. Then I heard some one call, 'You're shooting the wrong man; Scott is second in the line.' and ping! ping! the lead began to whistle about me. I rolled off the saddle, and, by the great horn spoon, what d'ye think of that—I had failed to load the magazine of my gun. Ought to have been killed, hadn't I?

"I know a bit about guns, and I heard five shots from my man, and then I knew that his magazine was out, and I started to run him down, but, happily, I thought better of it and made for a little arroyo and threw myself flat in it and plunked my magazine full of those long Mauser cartridges. Those are the boys I can get a man with at five miles' range. I raised up a bit and let drive at the puff of smoke where my man had fired at me, when bang! another fellow let drive at me and I got it in the leg.

"Say, you've heard the snare drummer at the theater start off a roll and keep it up? Well, that's the way our rifles and the other fellow's popped for a time.

"There was not much cover and it was every man for himself. We were not asleep, by any means.

"When it was all over I climbed on 'Slim' and started for Barstow, only 135 miles away. Yes, I felt rather bad. A bullet going 2560 feet a second doesn't add to your comfort on the desert when it strikes you and you have got to ride a mule to where there is a doctor.

" 'Slim' is just naturally wise. He knew there was a livery barn at Barstow, so we lit out. I had a bath towel with me and I tied it about my wound and rode sixty miles without water. Then we struck a water hole I knew and hot footed it on. I met a man seventy-five miles from Barstow and I offered him a goodly sum cold cash to take me in with his team. 'What's your name?' he asked me. 'Walter Scott,' I told him. 'Not on your life.' he said, 'for it would mean my life. I don't wish you any harm, but I know you are wanted by men who would kill me to kill you.' I had money but it was no good. I met another prospector and wanted to buy a bottle of whisky, but as soon as he learned I was Scott, he put the spurs to his mule and never looked back.

"I got into Barstow about sundown last night. 'Slim' pulled up in front of a saloon, and then I lost myself until I found I had been lifted off and laid on a pallet. I found a doctor then who gave me the first aid dope, and this morning I started for this place.

"You see that long ride in the cold, with the hole through my thigh was bad medicine. I haven't been able to eat anything since Sunday, and my stomach has bucked.

"How many of the men did we get? Say sonny, that's a story for them to tell. I'm not going into any details of an unpleasant nature. If they come back and have anything to say for themselves, all right! I'll make answer then.

"Who put them onto the game? I know all about it. I know who they are. I know how much they were paid. The money for them went through this city.

"I know their orders. These read: 'After you know where his claims are get the man.' and they tried their best, but we were just a little too much next to the business.

"They made a good campaign of it; I will do them that much justice. When they had us going, as they thought, they had triangulated us, there was a man with a rifle at each corner, and it was bing! bang! That's a good game in a gun fight, that triangle layout, and it might have won if we hadn't known the country and the business better."

THE OTHER FELLOWS

"No, I won't say a word about the results to the other fellows, nor who sent them after me. Time enough for that when some one else begins to talk. Up at Barstow the fellows said 'Scotty, we hope you bagged every one of them,' but that's something not necessary for publication just now, just as a guarantee of good faith, which is something I seem to have read in some blooming paper. I'm here, and where they are concerns them more than it does me."

Then Dr. Bayliss of the Angelus Hotel, who had been telephoned for, came in, and Scotty exhibited more of his wonderful nerve.

As the doctor undid the bandages of the wound, he said, "I won't hurt you more than I can help, but I want to probe this a bit to see if there is any danger of blood poisoning"

"Jab ahead," said Scott, "run the probe all the way through if you like; I've been as near death as I could be for a couple of days, and a little more pain don't count."

So while the doctor stuck his probe in the wound, Scotty laughed and joshed with his friends about his bed, and went over all the details of the fight.

"Being shot is not so bad," soliloquized Scotty, while the cruel probe was searching for his lacerated nerves, "but when you have to ride a mule 135 miles over the desert, and take your chances on getting water, it's bad medicine. I bled an awful lot, but I guess that was a good thing for it kept my wound clean. As I told you, money was no good out there. Every man I met dodged when I told him I was Scott. They knew there was a price on my head, and that they would likely get a bullet themselves if they were found in my company.

"No, they did not hit old Jackson, and Jack, my Indian, will get over his hurt all right. Will I go back? Cert, when I get over this. I've got my claims now so no one can take them, and if you were to count me down here on my bed $999,999. I would refuse it. They will bring me considerably over a million, unless those fellows get me—but they won't.

"Say, if you ever go on the desert and have men hunting you, the Dutch Mauser is the rifle to do the work. What work? Well, perhaps I'll tell you later. That is something I would rather have the fellows that shot at me tell.

"Can they tell it? Why, if they can talk they can."

"You are likely to get through this without much trouble," said Dr. Bayliss, as he wiped his malicious looking probes, and bound up the wound with anti-septic gauze. "You must stay in bed for three days, and if no pus develops you will come out all right. It was a high-power bullet that hit you, and those rarely carry any cloth into the wound they make."

Then the doctor sounded Scotty's lungs, and said that while he was suffering from his long exposure his splendid physique had carried him through wonderfully. Orders were given to have him left in quiet, and with that the friends filed out of the room.

The next day when Scott was again asked how the other fellows came out at Wind Gate Pass, he replied:—

"I'm no doctor," continuing he said.

"No, I won't talk about the results to the other fellows. We outplayed them—that's enough. If they come back and want to talk I'll talk myself.

"I'm not dodging any sheriffs, and I'll be ready with the dope.

"As a matter of fact I've got the right men spotted. I know all about their play. I know the man who sent them the money for the job; it went through a bank in this city. I know the telegrams they got, and their orders to kill me after they had spotted my claims. I've got the names of men they confided in.

"No, I won't say a word about what happened to them. You'll hear something about them pretty soon.

"I will say this though. I only fired three times. Did I hit my man? Now, son, when you're in a mix-up like that you don't keep tab of every bullet you send. Maybe we will hear more about it later."

CORK SCREW CANYON

The writer of this book has been in canyons in this country where they were very intricate. While they could be penetrated it was with difficulty that one got to their heads. One in particular known as Cork Screw Canyon and it was all and far more than the name implies. In order to get into the heart of the mountain and to the head of the canyon which did not lie possibly over one mile in from the mouth, one would have to travel twenty-five or thirty miles in order to gain the mile,—making several long detours around the heart—but gradually gaining on it—before winding up in the middle.

One advantage of this canyon, but an advantage that would lure one on, was the accessibility of the canyon. When I say the accessibility of the canyon I do not wish to contradict what I have said before. While it was intricate and hard to penetrate it was only so on account of a few by-canyons that branched off (more especially can this be said of the two outer circles) that would temporarily lead one astray—one not being able to tell them from the main canyon until brought to an abrupt end by a high towering wall in front.

This canyon is a regular mystic-maze, so to speak. And in making the outer detour or two, which are more oblong than the smaller and inner ones, one has to use all precaution possible upon again getting out of these by-canyons, or pockets, into which one gets side tracked, that one does not get back to his starting point. But as one first enters the canyon the heart of the mountain lies to the left so upon again getting out of these few small pockets, if one continually goes to the left he will gradually make the circuitous trip, after completing circle after circle around his final destination.

The canyon, easy of access, is as a rule only about 200

or 300 feet in width and in a great many places far less than that—high inspiring walls, thin and unsurmountable, are on either side. While the bed of the canyon is a gradual up grade, these perpendicular walls, nevertheless, even become higher as each detouring one gains on the inner recesses with its still higher walls. When one finally gains this inner fastness it is indeed inspiring. It being quite a spacious place with high perpendicular walls surrounding it. So near and yet so far to the outer world.

This mystic-maze Cork Screw Canyon, that one has to go so many miles in order to gain so few, was first shown to me by an old timer in the country—one who had been in the country for two decades and five years—and one who knew every peak, point and Indian trail throughout the entire system of mountain ranges.

There was even no Indian trail to guide one through this canyon—the entire mountain was held in superstition by them and consequently was not frequented.

While this canyon lies further east than "Mysterious Scott's" country is supposed to run, could it be, that he had a canyon something like this that was very intricate to all others than those who knew every point to guide them through the main canyon, into the fastnesses of the mountains? And did he also pad his burros' and mule's feet, as it was claimed, so as to leave no tell-tale marks behind? It evidently looks very much as though such is the case.

While numerous caches of his and what is supposed to be his main supply camp have been found, his mine has not been. "Camp Hold Out" is up an entirely different canyon. While it is an utter impossibility to gain "Camp Hold Out" only from the Death Valley side and it is then almost inaccessible, a mountain like the Cork Screw Canyon leads through, thrown up by nature in such a freakish manner, is even more seclusive a hiding place.

Is it in such a place as this that "Mysterious Scott's" source of wealth is held? Was it in such a place as this

"Mysterious Scott" was confined during the month of December—while upwards of a hundred were hunting for him? It is a mystery that the writer of this book can not solve.

IF I SHOULD DIE TONIGHT

If I should die tonight
    And you should come to my cold corpse and say,
    Weeping and heartsick o'er my lifeless clay—
If I should die tonight
    And you should come in deepest grief and woe—
    And say: "Here's that ten dollars that I owe,"
    I might arise in my white cravat
    And say: "What's that?"

If I should die tonight
    And you should come to my cold corpse and kneel,
    Clasping my bier to show the grief you feel,
I say, if I should die tonight
    And you should come to me, and there and then
    Just even hint 'bout payin' me that ten,
    I might arise the while,
    But I'd drop dead again.

                      —Ben King's Verse.

APPENDIX

Opportunities, New Strikes
... AND ...
Mining Review

This appendix is added not for the purpose of interesting capital—but for the purpose of giving those who would like to know more about the different sections of the country an opportunity to do so.

SPECIAL NOTICE

Many changes have taken place since the initial writing of this book. Far more are under course of construction and contemplation. It is hard to say what to-morrow has in store for the country. A prospect of to-day is liable to be a mine of to-morrow; an idea of to-day, a reality of to-morrow.

The railroad to Tonopah has been pushed on to Goldfield and new road built so as to connect with main line of the Southern Pacific at Hazen instead of at Reno; all of it has been made standard gauge and through service with Pullman sleepers and dining cars from Goldfield direct to San Francisco installed. This railroad—the Tonopah and Goldfield—has already the rolling stock on hand and has made survey and is to continue building to Rhyolite. Two other roads are at the present writing building from the south also to that district. The Tonopah and Tidewater is building from the new Clark road from Las Vegas, ultimately to Tonopah, while from the Santa Fe, "Borax" Smith is building from Ludlow, California, to the Bullfrog District, via his Lila C. mine—having a great number of miles graded and track laid for part of it.

A 100-stamp mill is being erected at Tonopah for the purpose of treating its ores.

Bishop Creek, California, which has an immense power going to waste, has been harnessed by a company, known as the Nevada Power, Mine and Milling Co., and part of its power transmitted a distance of 98 miles to Goldfield and an additional 28 miles to Tonopah, so as to give a cheap power for the treating of ores—2,000 h.p. has already been installed and at this time new reservoirs are being constructed and an additional 2,000 h. p. is being put in. Large stone distributing stations are built at Tonopah by this power company and it is their intention to also build stations in Bullfrog District and Silver Peak.

Railroad Day in Goldfield was September 14th, 1905, and this electric power was turned on September 17th. It was a great week for Goldfield as it means cheaper freight rates and cheaper power.

Goldfield has five different stamp mills already completed, besides a Sampling Ore Co. for sampling and buying of ore, and three other mills are being constructed and will be finished shortly by the Combination people,—an additional 10 stamps to their already 10-stamp mill—the Sandstorm people and the Jumbo people.

Goldfield, which had a half dozen tents in November, 1903, has become quite a metropolitan city. Some stone business blocks are being erected and many nice residences for a city of its age. Among other conveniences can be named electric lights, good newspapers, churches, a gentlemen's social club of 175 members and a healthy Mining Exchange which has been inaugurated to trade in Tonopah, Goldfield and Bullfrog stocks.

In the Bullfrog District each one of the principal cities has a first-class hotel and a good newspaper. All the towns are amply supplied with water. Beatty and Gold Center being on the Amargosa, can get water at a few feet, while each of the other two towns have a water supply of their own—mains being laid on all the streets in the cities, besides the third system is being put in now, for milling and other purposes. Daily stages, carrying U. S. mail, enter this section from Goldfield on the north, and from Las Vegas, on the Salt Lake route on the south—besides automobiles are continuously in service in all directions. An electric light plant is being put up. Local telephone system has been installed with a goodly number of customers; two ice plants,—one at Beatty and another at Bullfrog, besides a third one going up at Gold Center in connection with a brewery.

A 20-stamp mill is being put up at Gold Center and two more companies are organized for the immediate construction of two more stamp mills in the Bullfrog District. These things together with three railroads building to this section do not speak bad for a camp one year old

OPPORTUNITIES

Is Nevada at last being inhabited? People heretofore have been robbing her of her riches and have gone elsewhere to live.

The Comstock alone has to its credit of making more multi-millionaires than any other mining property—the enormous sum of from six hundred to seven hundred millions of dollars having been taken out of that property.

The new strikes in the state have made a record of their own for the time of discovery—a record second to none for a strike of its age.

It looks as though the days of Virginia City and the old Comstock are to be repeated. Tonopah, Goldfield, and Bullfrog were discovered within four years' time. Many other recent important strikes have been made. There are other Tonopahs; there are other Goldfields; there are other Bullfrogs as yet undiscovered within the confines of the numerous mountain ranges throughout the state. These mountains many of them haven't more than been looked at—let alone being prospected.

There are very few who are living to-day who will see Nevada's hills thoroughly prospected. It will be months and possibly years before it can be said even—"The hills around Goldfield and in the Bullfrog District are thoroughly prospected," as they are far from it at the present.

Nevada is attracting mining experts from all over the world; they pronounce it good. Many say it is the best mineralized section known of to-day. This is what Charles M. Schwab who has bought extensive interests in Nevada mining properties said, at a reception recently, of Nevada's outlook:

"I believe Nevada is destined to be one of the greatest states in the union, and in saying this I only give expression to a thought which I have often uttered. During the past twenty years the great fortunes of this country have been made in manufacturing. I believe the next twenty years are going to see the great fortunes of this country made from the mineral deposits of these United States—and if any part of this country has been well provided with minerals, Southern Nevada has."

He has backed this up by investments.

The field for prospectors, with some cash, or for the investor both in stocks and in mines, is good and will be good for many a year to come yet—both in the new camps and the unprospected territory. There was never a mine in the United States no matter how many millions it might have become worth soon afterwards, but what at one time in its history a few dollars would have secured title. The mining industry, especially until the ore is blocked out, is more or less a game of chance—but every business has that element in it. Go into it the same as any other business deal. Use common every-day judgment and caution; management has much to do with the property. While it is a chance—see that the percentage is in your favor on the go-in, so as to get a good run for your money, and I dare say, if you follow these rules, you will be a winner in your mining speculations.

There is no excuse for "wild catting" in Nevada to-day. I have no doubt but what some has been attempted but it is not necessary—as there are enough properties with merit, either as to surface showing or extra good location, to work on. The man that goes into "wild catting" to-day in Nevada would sooner make a dishonest dollar than an honest one, or he is too lazy to try and keep posted as to the meritorious propositions.

Why has this state been overlooked by man? Why has it been dormant, especially can that be said for the last twelve years?

These are questions that present themselves to Easterners. They are easily answered by one who is on the ground to-day. It has been no "pleasure trip" for the prospector to pioneer the country. Water, while it is quite plentiful, is hard to locate. The water from the springs, and many of them are large ones, as a rule only flows for a few hundred feet before again sinking into the ground. It has been a costly proposition heretofore for the prospector. He would have to have a fair sum or he could not prospect. The first spring and summer in the Bullfrog District with far better railroad facilities than in years prior and where freighting was made a business to a large nucleus of people, the cost of some of the commodities were as follows:— Lumber, $130 to $150 per M; shingles, $12 per M; nails, $12\frac{1}{2}$c lb.; hay, $100 per ton; barley, 8c per lb.; eggs, 75c per dozen; flour, $4.50 per 50 lbs.; gasoline, $4 per five gal.; coal oil, $3.50 per five gal.; potatoes, 8c per lb., etc. With these prices prevailing after good sized towns are established, one can judge for himself what these commodities were worth to the lone gold seeker before these camps were thought of. That, together with requiring a season's trip to locate springs so as to prospect to good advantage—was a handicap that was sufficient to bar him from investigating into the mineral resources of the state— little was it thought that it held the riches that it does. If mines were found there would have been the long haul for freighting.

Prior to the recent extensive rich gold strikes Nevada was considered a silver state. The depreciation of silver in 1893 caused capital to look elsewhere than to Nevada for mining investments. These recent gold strikes, the almost simultaneous advent of the San Pedro, Los Angeles, Salt Lake Railroad through the southern part of the state with the present building of branches from different directions by all the railroads, together with more modern mining machinery, is giving—and is going to give—Nevada a revival that is justified.

RECLAIMING THE DESERT

The fore part of this year, June 17, 1905, witnessed the finishing of the first project under the Reclamation Act—it being also the third anniversary of the signing of that Act by the President—an Act to reclaim the arid lands of our vast domain under National Irrigation.

This date meant more to Nevada than to any other state as it is the first to get national irrigation. It was upon that date that the Truckee-Carson irrigation project was partially completed and celebrated—and forms the commencement of a new epoch in Nevada's history—an epoch of homes and permanency.

The Truckee River has a bountiful supply of water. The Carson Valley has a vast expanse of flat thirsty land that is good for irrigation, far more than can be irrigated by its own river. The combining of the water of these two rivers and putting it on these arid flat lands of the Carson Valley was the part of the Government. It was a big project. It required a big outlay of capital, but with the vast amount of money that the Government has at its command it was possible to see its realization.

A canal was built, thirty-one miles in length, to convey this water from the Truckee River to the Carson Valley. This canal there empties the water into a large storage reservoir. This reservoir is designed to have a capacity of 286,000 acre feet, or, in other words, to hold enough water to cover that many acres a depth of one foot. The water flows from this reservoir into the channel of the Carson River—a distance of four and one-half miles further—to the diversion dam, which is at the head of the irrigation system, where the combined waters of the two rivers there, by two large canals—one on each side of the river—irrigate the land.

At the date of the celebration of the opening of the headgate and partial completion of the project—June 17th—there were 40,000 acres of land under these canals ready for settlement. The ultimate length of the two main canals will be upwards of ninety miles, while with the laterals and drainage ditches in Carson Valley alone, which only comprise part of the project, will be over 1,200 miles, and in less than three years' time there will be 200,000 acres ready for settlement with ultimately from 300,000 to 400,000 acres in this valley.

This land can be taken up by the Homestead Act—in tracts from forty to one-hundred and sixty acres according to location, character of soil, roughness of surface and irrigability. The cost of the land per acre will be according to the cost of the irrigation project—and gives the numerous homesteaders several years to reimburse the Government.

L. H. Tyler, the Government Engineer for Nevada, under the Reclamation Service, gave out the following report at that time as to the work:

Work on the main Truckee canal, designed to carry the Truckee river water from a point twenty-four miles east of Reno, a distance of thirty-one miles, to the Carson river, was begun in April, 1903. This canal has a capacity for the first six miles of 1400 cubic feet per second, and for the remainder of its course of 1200 cubic feet per second. The depth of water will be thirteen feet. The width at the top varies from twenty-four to sixty-three feet. Nearly two miles of the canal, exclusive of tunnels, are lined with concrete. The main Truckee canal will discharge its waters into the Carson river at the site of the lower Carson reservoir. Thence the water flows in a channel of that stream about four and a half miles to the diversion dam at the head of the distributing system. This dam directs the water into two main distributing canals on either side of the Carson river. That on the south has a bed width of twenty-two feet and a top width of twenty-eight feet, and carries twelve feet of water. The north side canal is thirteen feet wide at the bottom, forty-five feet wide at the top, and carries six and a half feet of water. These two canals are completed for thirty-eight miles. With their main branches they will ultimately have a total length of over ninety miles, while the laterals and drain ditches to be constructed in the Carson Sink valley alone will aggregate fully 1,200 miles. Already nearly 200 miles of these have been finished, and before the end of July, 1905, nearly 300 miles now under construction will be ready for use, and will distribute water to 50,000 acres of land.

This part of the irrigation system comprises the most difficult and expensive portion of the initial item of the Truckee-Carson project, and when finished will have cost about $1,750,000. The extensions of this—in Carson Sink valley, completing the initial item, and bringing under irrigation not less than 200,000 acres of land—will increase the total expense to about $2,600,000 and consume about two years' time.

Further extensions of the Truckee-Carson project to a total area of, approximately, 375,000 acres of land, involve the construction of expensive storage reservoirs and costly high-line canals. This work has been planned, however, and as the lands to be immediately watered are being rapidly taken by homeseekers, funds for the completion of the work will be provided by the payments to be made on the water rights therefor. It is estimated that the entire undertaking can thus be completed within nine years, the total cost being estimated at approximately $9,000,000.

The number of acres of land ultimately designed to be irrigated is from 300,000 to 400,000 acres, of which 200,000 will be supplied within the next three years. Of this acreage it is estimated that about 40,000 acres will be irrigated during the present year.

The land is located in a number of valleys along the Truckee and Carson rivers, extending on each side from the Central Pacific Railroad, the distance being in some places twenty-five miles from the road.

The main body of 200,000 acres to be irrigated first is in the Carson Sink valley, south of the railroad. Some of this land is immediately adjacent, while the farthest extends about twenty-five miles from the railway.

The soil is adapted to alfalfa, all forage crops, potatoes, onions, beets, and other vegetables, apples, pears, berries and other hardier deciduous fruits. The soil and climate are similar to those in the vicinity of Salt Lake and Ogden.

The public lands are subject to entry under the homestead act, no price being charged for the land, but the cost of irrigation will be assessed against the land as a charge for the water right, to be repaid in ten annual installments without interest, at the rate of $2.60 per annum per acre. This covers the cost of maintenance and operation during the ten-year period, and provides for the delivery of water to each farm, and also for a comprehensive drainage system.

After the ten-year period stated, the land and water rights belong to the holders of the lands forever, with no further charge by the Government. The care and maintenance of the system then passes into the hands of the land owners, under laws, however, made for the purpose which will insure protection against corporate or individual greed and fraud.

The public lands are now open to entry under the homestead act, but intending settlers are strongly advised not to file upon any of the lands outside of the district to be irrigated during the current year, and not until we can inform them when the water will be ready for delivery to such outside lands, for the reason that, without water they can produce nothing which will yield them a living.

Any unmarried person over 21 years of age, or any head of a family, who is, or has declared intention to become, a citizen of the United States, who has not used his or her homestead right, or who is not then owner of more than 160 acres of land in any state, can file on any one of these tracts. Title to land cannot be acquired until all payments for water have been made. The law requires a homesteader to see and select his land personally

Residence must be established on land within six months after filing thereon, and must be continuous thereafter and the land cultivated for the term of five years.

The cost of water to settlers has been fixed at $26 per acre irrigable, payable in ten equal annual installments, without interest.

The climate is mild and dry and the elevation is about 4,000 feet above sea level. With this healthful mountainous climate, with these arid lands amply supplied with water, there will come a transition that is hard to believe. Thrifty and prosperous farms and villages will be, in a very short space of time, located where heretofore there has been a barren waste.

The above is just one of the irrigation projects that Nevada will see in the course of a few years. It is thought that the state has a large underflow of water. It is singular but it is nevertheless true—none of Nevada's rivers flow out of the state—none of them reach the ocean unless it is by an underground flow. It is thought by many that artesian wells could be bored and an abundance of water secured for irrigation purposes.

Luther Burbanks, termed the "Wizard of Horticulture," has given to the world a spineless cactus that he, with the aid of nature, is perfecting. This cactus is noted for its food qualities both for man and animal. Will it not be possible and at not a distant day to see a large amount of the more level lands cultivated and to see cattle and sheep in countless numbers grazing or feeding on this cactus on our more rough and unwatered lands?

I'll leave the above question for others to solve—but, many think time will see Nevada an agricultural state as well as ranking first in precious metals—that a Rip Van

Winkle taking a nap on Nevada territory to-day, will, upon awaking up, believe he has been transported to the Garden of Eden during his slumber.

SOME MORE RECENT STRIKES

One of the new and principal strikes during midsummer this year, 1905, was made in what is now known as the Wild Rose Mining District by Peter Augurbury, commonly known as "French Pete."

The rock was found within twenty feet of a trail that has been used for the last forty years—one leading from Death Valley to Ballarat, California, via Black Water.

He camped there for dinner—picked up a piece of float that looked good to him, broke it open, finding free gold sticking out of it. He afterwards went up the mountain and located the lead.

"Shorty" Harris and I. T. Davis were on the scene at the time of the strike and all three were successful in securing good claims. Mr. Augurbury located nineteen claims for himself and his associates, while Mr. Davis and "Shorty" Harris, for themselves and their associates, each staked seventeen and fourteen claims respectively. Many high assays have been secured, some running from $900 to $1,500 per ton, practically from the surface. A town has been started and named Harrisburg, located in California, about twenty-eight miles north of Ballarat.

Among other important strikes, in which high values were secured, and to which there were stampedes for, can be named: Silver Bow, in Kawich Range, twenty-eight miles north of Kawich; Happy Hooligan, fourteen miles west of Rhyolite; Manhattan, near Sodaville, and Stone Cabin in the Kawich Range. The first two named were made prior to the Wild Rose strike, the latter two since then.

MINING REVIEW

In getting this mining review, the writer visited each of the districts enumerated, and with a very few exceptions, had the pleasure of visiting each of the properties.

He was unable to take in Montezuma, Silver Peak, and Lida on the west of Goldfield, all of which are old camps and have some extra good properties, and his travels also did not include the newer camps of Kawich and Silver Bow on the east.

Just a few of the properties in each district are enumerated—for instance, in the Tonopah District every property mentioned is a shipper, the same thing can practically be said of Goldfield, while in the Bullfrog District but very few have been named where ore of good value has not been encountered as yet. These few so enumerated are properties that have some work done and from their location there is every reason to believe that they stand a very good chance to encounter the ledges that are on adjoining properties.

If a property is not mentioned in this review—as it is only a partial one—it is no sign that it is not of great merit—possibly it shows up far more than some other property that is mentioned. Besides that class of properties that have struck good values, and are not mentioned there are dozens of others that lie in close proximity to ones of great merit in each of these districts that have no work done on them otherwise than the location and assessment work. What a little work with pick, shovel and powder will reveal is hard to say.

The write-up of the mines in districts south of the Bullfrog District is under date of September 1st; Bullfrog District, October 1st; Goldfield and Tonopah Districts, November 1st, 1905.

APPENDIX

TONOPAH DISTRICT

The first property in the Tonopah District was staked off in August, 1900. James L. Butler, who was at that time District Attorney for Nye County, cut out towards the south from Belmont in May to prospect this district. One night he camped at a spring—known to the Indians as Tonopah—which translated means—"Water near the surface." The next morning while looking for his burros he ran across—about four miles from the spring—these ledges from which he took several samples of rock. This same rock (the ledges from which it was taken have since produced many millions of dollars and it is said that ten times as much is to-day blocked out as has been produced) was knocked around, assayers not thinking enough of it to think it worthy of treating. When it was finally run through, several assays made and the results were all from $80.00 to $600.00 per ton values—Mr. Butler being apprised of it, returned together with his wife to the section in August and staked out a group of claims, being those of the Tonopah Mining Company. While Mr. Butler was staking out a claim on one side of the mountain, Mrs. Butler was staking out another on the other side, which she named the Mizpah, meaning, "The Lord watch between me and thee, while we are absent one from the other." This claim has since become famous as a producer.

Tonopah gets better with age. Three years ago it was considered a one mine camp, since then there has been seven or eight mines discovered that are regular shippers, besides good prospects of several others being brought into the regular shippers class as development work goes on.

Up to August of last year, Sodaville on the Carson and Colorado Railroad, a distance of 62 miles, was the nearest point to railroad. The Tonopah Railroad which was completed at that time was originally a narrow gauged one but has been reconstructed into a standard gauged one this past summer and through service installed.

A 100-stamp mill is also being constructed so as to treat the ores of the numerous mines instead of shipping to a great distance also corraling of Bishop Creek, California, —120 miles distant and its power transmitted to this district gives cheaper power.

(*NOVEMBER 1st, 1905*)

The Tonopah Mining Company of Nevada owns eight claims lying on the western slope of Mt. Oddie. This group was the first located in the Tonopah District— the famous Mizpah claim of this group being located by Mrs. James Butler. Over $10,000,000 has already been taken from this property and it is estimated that there is over $100,000,000 in sight. Many leasers have made vast fortunes from the property on a one year lease.

The underground workings consist of from five to six miles of shafts. drifts and cross-cuts. The deepest shaft is the Mizpah shaft—a triple compartment one—which is down to the depth of 950 feet. The Valley View shaft from which the working of the Valley View vein is being operated is down to a depth of 700 feet. This vein is as large as that of the original Mizpah vein. The Red Plume shaft is a new three compartment one down 400 feet—from which point they are cross-cutting.

The property is owned by Philadelphia parties and a 100-stamp mill is being erected. The stamp mill and the new electric hoists which are being installed at this time will be run by electric power, generated by steam The same plant will also furnish power for the new sampler of the Western Ore Purchasing Co., which is being built near the power station, fourteen miles westerly on the line of the new Tonopah-Goldfield Railroad.

The stock of the Tonopah Mining Co. is selling at about $13.50 per share. During this year three dividends of twenty-five cents per share each have been paid, or a disbursement of $750,000 to the stock holders for that time.

The Tonopah Extension Mining Co. owns a group of claims lying in the flat at the foot of Mt. Oddie and on the continuation of the Mizpah ledge. The property is owned by Pittsburg people—among the main stockholders being Charles M. Schwab and John Y. McKane. It is considered second to none in the district outside of the Tonopah (Mizpah) Mining Co. The main shaft is down 600 feet and lowest level run is at the 500 foot—levels also at the 300 and the 400 foot. The veins are from six to sixteen feet in width and are mainly sulphides.

This property has been a dividend payer for some time, it having paid $150,000 in dividends in the last six months, besides making wonderful surface improvements. It is said to have $40,000,000 in sight untouched as yet. The stock is around the $6 per share mark. A new stone office building has just been completed and the mine is equipped with strictly modern machinery. The mine has installed a 15-drill compressor, 200 h. p. boilers, machine shops, etc. being capable of doing all necessary mechanical work at the property.

The Montana=Tonopah Mining Co. consists of fifteen claims and three fractions lying north of the Tonopah, west of the North Star, and east of the Midway, adjoining them. The main shaft is down about 800 feet and there is upwards of two and a half miles of underground workings with a great amount of ore blocked out—the largest veins being that of the MacDonald and the South ledges.

At the present writing the company is installing improvements to the extent of $30,000 to $40,000, among them being a new gallows frame, electric hoist and compressor.

This property is a regular shipper, but as there is so much silicious ore that the present smelter capacity cannot handle only a small percentage of it, their shipments are curtailed to about thirty tons per day, consequently the main work has to be confined to that of development. This Company was the first to declare a dividend in the camp.

The Tonopah-Bellmont Development Co. consists of about twelve claims—lying on the east side of the Tonopah Mining Co.—taking in the south side of Mt. Oddie. The main shaft is down 1,100 feet and 7,000 feet of development work has been done. This development work cuts several large veins—the extension of the veins found originally on the Tonopah, Montana and North Star groups. This is one of the new mines just being developed and is a big producer, shipping from 300 to 400 tons per week. The chief owners of this property are Philadelphia people, and are the same, as a rule, as the owners of the Tonopah Mining Co.

The Tonopah=Midway Mining Co. owns five claims lying west of the Montana and north of the Tonopah. The main shaft is 650 feet in depth with 5,000 feet of development work most of which is on the 550 foot level, also on the 450 foot. The veins on this property range from nine to eleven feet and in places to fifteen feet in width. This property is shipping from sixty to ninty tons per week right along—development work only being done—no stoping having been done as yet.

The treasury is in good shape and it is only a matter of time before it becomes a regular dividend payer. They could pay a good dividend now, but are waiting until more ore is blocked out so as to miss no dividends after starting.

The Tonopah Extension Mining and Milling Co., commonly known as the "West End,"—consists of one full claim lying west of the Tonopah and south of the

MacNamara—it being near the heart of the City of Tonopah.

The double compartment shaft is down 780 feet in depth with levels run on the 200, 400, and 500 foot—and are working on the 400 foot level at present. In sinking the shaft they encountered a quartz ledge, through which they have sunk 300 feet—as no foot wall has been found as yet, they do not know the size of the ledge. It is more than probable the Valley View ledge of the Tonopah. All the work up to date has been done for development only, no stoping having been done. It is the intention of the company to be a regular shipper from now on as they have lots of ore in sight and have started making shipments. "Borax" Smith is one of the main owners of this property.

The North Star Tunnel and Development Co. consists of a group of claims lying directly east of the Montana end-lining with it and lying further up on Mt. Oddie than the Montana.

The double compartment shaft is down 1,100 feet with levels run at 950 feet and 1,050 feet—and at 700 feet a cross-cut connects the property with the 500 foot level of the Montana.

This property is one of the regular shippers of the camp and a few days previous to the writer's visit while making an upraise from the 950 foot level to the 750 level, a body of rich ore was encountered—assays showing 1,460 oz. silver and 20 oz. gold. The ore on this property is very similar to that of the Montana.

The Jim Butler Tonopah Mining Co. comprises a group of sixteen claims—a few fractions among them—lying south and east and immediately adjoining the Tonopah. It is owned by practically the same people as the Tonopah, mainly Philadelphia people, and is under the same management as the Tonopah. There are six shafts on this property varying from 400 to 600 feet in depth. Upon the writer's visit he found most of the workings being done through the Wander Boy shaft—shipping ore being placed on the dump. They have a great amount of territory and part of the town site of Tonopah lies on a portion of it.

The Golden Anchor Mining Co. consists of a group of claims owned by the Schwab-McKane Syndicate. The main shaft is to a depth of 850 feet. As there was no one in authority at the property to show the writer through upon his visit he cannot go into detail as to its workings, but it is generally known that several large ledges have been encountered. It is expected to join the list of regular shippers in a very short time.

The MacNamara Mining Co. consists of one claim lying north of the West End, south of the Tonopah Extension and west of the Tonopah. The full two compartment shaft is down 500 feet with levels at 200, 300, 350 and 500 feet. The ledge is a large one and the development work has blocked out quite a quantity of ore. This property has shipped some high grade ore.

The Ohio Tonopah Mining Co. owns five claims and five fractions lying south of the Tonopah Extension and west of the MacNamara and the West End.

The main shaft is down 780 feet with stations cut at the 200, 500, and 600 feet with drifts and cross-cuts mainly on the 400 and 700 foot levels. A body of low grade ore has been encountered but no shipments made.

THE GOLDFIELD DISTRICT

The Goldfield District is a world beater for its age. In November, 1903, the camp had a half dozen newly put-up tents; to-day it is quite a metropolitan city of 10,000 population—and the camp is in its infancy. The first year's output of ore amounted to upwards of four millions of dollars—more than Cripple Creek's first four years—the second will record a large output with a vast number of millions in sight.

The following companies are operating mills and treating the ores:—Oddie and Gardner; The Combination; The New Western Co.; The American Reduction Co.; The H. L. Frank Mill; and the Columbia Sampling Ore Co;—besides the Combination is increasing theirs an additional 10-stamps and the Sandstorm and the Jumbo companies are each building at the present time. Leases are again being given; the Tonopah railroad has been built to Goldfield; and Bishop Creek harnessed and electric power carried to the District. The railroad was finished September 14th and the other project completed a few days later.

It might be said that the district as now defined is divided into four sections—one lying east of Goldfield, one-half mile, and south of Columbia Mountain in which many bonanza properties are located,—another section north of Columbia Mountain, among these properties is the Sandstorm and Kendall—the Diamondfield Section, five miles northeast of the city, and the Knickerbocker Mountain Section, three miles east.

(*NOVEMBER 1st, 1905*)

The Florence Goldfield Mining Co. own four claims, lying southeast of the Combination and southwest of the Jumbo, between these two properties.

This is conceded to be one of the bonanza properties—if not the bonanza property of the camp. Already over a million and a half dollars of ore has been taken out by leasers on this property. One lease—the Reilly-McKane-Campbell lease has been the recent talk of the town. This lease terminated the 17th of October—just 76 days after the high pay streak was encountered. During those 76 days, several days production ran as high as $20,000 per day, while the entire 76 days approximately averaged $10,000 per day making a grand sum of three-quarters of a million dollars for the short time to the expiration of the lease. Another lease, a previous one, together with the sub-leases have taken out even a larger amount than the Reilly-McKane-Campbell lease. The company has started to work this recently expired lease (Reilly lease) and at the time of the writer's visit they were sampling the vein from top to bottom. It was their intention to take 1,000 samples and assays—upwards of 400 had been taken at that time. The company workings had up to the time of the expiration of this lease been confined to the developing of the property from the point where the previous leasers had to let go. This work lies to the south, some distance from the Reilly lease.

From the time the writer entered the shaft on the surface to the time he reappeared, he was in the ore vein the entire distance. These workings of the company, through which the writer went, from one end to the other, consists of 3,800 feet of under ground work, besides some stoping,—all of which is in a ledge from 14 to 18 feet in width, which carries values in its entirety. The shaft is 350 feet deep with extensive drifts on ledge, and numerous cross-cuts exposing the width, on the 100, 150, 200, 250, 300, and 350 foot levels. As one enters the drift on the 100 foot level—the vein which is a well defined one, can readily be seen. It is about fourteen feet in width on this level. The vein here is drifted on 400 feet with various cross-cuts showing width. On the other levels the drifting was still more extensive with numerous cross-cuts. About twenty feet above the 150 foot level the vein changes from the oxidized ore to the sulphites, it also widens to about eighteen feet. The extra high pay streak which is from six inches to three feet in width, runs enormously rich while the entire balance of the fourteen to eighteen foot vein runs from $30 to $40 ore. The last shipment the company made ran $2,002 per ton, it going 100.8 oz. gold, balance silver and copper. It was encountering this rich pay shoot that made the leases so profitable. Quite a bit of stoping has been done from the 150 foot to the 200 foot level. The company, at the time of the writer's visit was working on these levels on this vein, and as it is the same kind of ore as Reilly encountered further north and the trend on the different levels was making directly towards the Reilly workings, it is without doubt the same vein as Reilly encountered. It is the intention of the company to continue developing on vein until the two workings are connected. They were also replacing the 25 h. p. gasoline hoist with a 50 h. p. electric, preparatory to carrying this work on faster and also to sinking lower.

The Jumbo Mining Co., of Goldfield, owns about four claims, or rather 65 acres, lying south of the Red Top and east of the Florence, side-lining with the latter. It has been one of the bonanza producers of the camp. Leasers during the leasing period upon this property took out $1,500,000 in a very short time. On account of a very slight wrangle for control of minor consequence between the Taylors and another faction, little work has been done on the property since the leasers time was up January 1st,

1905. Whatever differences there might have been has recently been cleared away and again work has been resumed. The recent workings have been confined to again getting the property in ship-shape order, the leasers not having left it in such, and sinking the shaft to a deeper depth. It is 430 feet deep at the present writing and it is the intention to go to the 500 foot level before cross-cutting. A stamp mill is also being installed on the property. As stated before the work is being done in workmanlike manner and property put in shape.

Besides the Jumbo lead the Red Top lead extends across the property 2,000 feet besides other cross-leads that carry very good values.

The Taylors—Harry Taylor and Charles Taylor, who are large owners in this property, the first mentioned being the superintendent—staked the first claim south of Columbia Mountain. They staked this property and the Florence one afternoon. As these two properties have produced over three million dollars, under leasers, in a very short period and the properties are practically untouched as yet, it is not considered a bad half-day's work.

The Combination Mines Co. owns ten full claims and three fractions—divided into two groups about one-half mile apart. Most of the workings have been confined to the north group, it being in the midst of the territory that has taken out the extremely large values—it having the January and February claims of the Goldfield Mining Co. on one side and the Jumbo and Florence properties on the other. On this group the main shaft is down approximately 350 feet in depth with a great amount of development work on the various levels done. This property was originally sold to the present company for the small sum of $75,000. It is said that the owners only had to go into their pockets for $10,000., balance was taken out of the mine in digging a 75 foot shaft, before the second payment was due.

The mine besides paying for itself, also the installing of the modern 10-stamp mill, piping its water for a distance of twelve miles, has been paying a dividend each month of $40,000 for the last eleven months. Besides the 10-stamp mill already installed another 10 stamps is being put in at this time by this company. As it is capitalized at $400,000, this property is paying over 120% per annum on its capitalization, and several times that per cent over its real cost to its present owners.

The Goldfield Mining Co. owns seven claims in all, divided into three groups. One group consisting of the January and February claims, lies due west and immediately adjoining the Combination Mines Co.—sidelining with it—another group, three claims, lies south of the Florence property while the other two claims lie north of Columbia Mountain a few feet east of the Sandstorm property.

Development work has been confined mainly to the first group mentioned, consisting of the January and February claims. On these claims, and more especially on the January claim, leasers and the owners have taken out a large amount of money, it running above the $750,000 mark. The main shaft at present is 300 feet in depth with extensive cross-cuts and drifts at the various levels. Several leasers are at work on the February claim. Some of these leasers have made shipments of some high grade ore with good prospects of striking it in large bodies on this claim as well as on the January.

The Red Top Mining Co. owns one and a fraction claims lying north of the Jumbo property and end-lining with it. The ledge which extends the entire length of the property, is a well defined one which can readily be seen on the surface for 200 rods, it also extending over onto the Jumbo property. There are four shafts on property—three by leasers and one by the company. There is one unexpired lease still operating. No new leases are being let, I believe. The company's shaft is a full two compartment one and is as nice a shaft as the writer has had the pleasure of seeing in the newer gold fields, it being thoroughly timbered from top to bottom It is 180 feet in depth with work done on three levels—50, 100, and 165 foot levels. There are cross-cuts to ledge from each level and drifts run on the ledge, or more properly speaking on the richer pay shoot, on the various levels. This pay shoot, which can be readily seen, is drifted on 100 feet on the 50 foot level, 500 feet on the 100 level, with raise on the lead from the 100 foot level, 45 degree pitch, to the 50 foot level. This raise is all on the rich pay shoot which is large ledge from eighteen inches to eight feet in width, many assays have been made that run almost the $7,000 mark. On the 50 foot level this pay shoot is about two feet in width besides which there are 15 feet in width of ore that runs $25 to the ton; on the 165 foot level there are 100 feet of cross-cuts, besides 300 foot drift on pay shoot. On this—the lowest level—they have about 40 feet in width of milling ore besides this pay shoot. There are upwards of 400 feet of cross-cuts on the various levels.

There were from 500 to 600 tons of shipping ore sacked on dump ready for shipment. This was just secured in development work, while they have 235 feet of stoping ground above their lowest level, no stoping has been done as yet.

(Since writing the above article and before the finishing of this review another very rich strike has been made on this property).

Goldfield C. O. D. Mining Co. owns 58 acres lying south of the Florence. One shipment by leasers has been made, running $189.40 per ton. Little work has been done as yet on this property and the shipment was from outcroppings. This property has changed hands recently and development work on a large scale is about to be commenced.

The Gold Bar consists of a fraction lying due east of the C. O. D. property and is owned by practically the same parties, mainly Pittsburg people. It records two shipments—the ore running $105 per ton, screenings $35.

Development work consists of shaft 68 feet deep with drift on vein 70 feet, eastward. The rich pay streak had just been encountered again at that depth but at the time of the writer's visit the returns from the assayers had not as yet been secured. At present, on this and the C. O. D. property is the furthest south ore has been encountered in this district.

The St. Ives consists of seventeen acres lying due east of the Jumbo. Main shaft is to a depth of 275 feet besides others of a lesser depth—one 90 foot, where quite a bit of ore has been taken out. Cross-cuts and drifts have been run on the various levels. Values have been encountered but are going after the high grade vein. $10,000 by leasers was taken out of property. Operations on a more extensive scale are soon to be resumed.

The Velvet Gold Mining Co. owns three claims lying due east of the Jumbo at a distance of 100 feet, also east of the St. Ives, side-lining with it. This property shipped from $10,000 to $12,000 of high grade ore, which laid practically on the surface. Developing of the property is now going on on the Algea claim near the St. Ives. A 50 foot shaft has been sunk, at base of ridge, and from that level they are tunnelling into the mountain with good indications of encountering values. One or two leases are also being worked on the property.

The Blue Bull Mining Co. owns eight claims lying south of the Simmerone fraction and west of the Commonwealth—being about one and a half miles due east of Goldfield. The company's main workings consist of about 400 feet of surface work besides shaft 120 feet in depth. One leaser is to a depth of 130 feet, besides cross-cuts, etc. This leaser is in vein from which he secured assay running 46% lead, 11 oz. in silver and 1½ oz. in gold. There is more or less showing on all parts of ground.

The Goldfield Commonwealth Mining Co owns eleven claims immediately adjoining and to the east of the Lone Star. Simmerone fraction and the Blue Bull. Main development work consists of shaft on Commonwealth, No. 3, claim about 80 feet in depth. The shaft is sunk on a large vein fourteen or fifteen feet in width and drifting has been started at bottom of shaft all being in vein, exposing a great amount of milling ore. On the Tokop claim a tunnel has been run for a distance of 400 feet cross-cutting numerous veins and on the same claim there is a shaft down thirty feet in depth—bottom of which is in shipping ore. There are several sets of leasers working on the group all of whom have more or less of a good showing and fair indications of encountering large values.

The Sandstorm Section—Goldfield District

The Sandstorm Mining Co. consists of four full claims lying about one and a half miles north of Goldfield, being on the north side of Columbia Mountain. This and the Kendall property were the first to be located in the Goldfield district and the section was first known as the Grandpa District.

The Sandstorm has gone to a depth of 135 feet. The shaft followed the ledge down 97 feet and it is the intention to cross-cut to the ledge in a day or two. This property has recorded approximately $150,000 production—it all being taken out by leasers and above the 44 foot level. The company's workings are the continuation of the leasers and have been for development work only. The company expects to take out more this month than all previous outputs. There is one lease still in operation on the property and is producing shipments of high grade ore.

The Kendall Goldfield Mining Co. owns three claims lying directly north of the Sandstorm and adjoining it. The development work consists of various shafts and cross-cuts. The main shaft is down 230 feet with cross-cuts from the 60 foot—two from the 80 foot and one on the 100 foot levels.

The property records a production to date of $200,000. One shipment of fifteen tons paid the company $75,000 and it looks as though such shipments as that will soon be almost lost sight of, as a couple of recent strikes on this property the last few days is the talk of the camp. One shaft that is down thirty feet on a five foot ledge has encountered ore that is expected, by a very conservative estimation, to run upwards of $2,000 per ton. As this ore is taken out it is being sacked and is being placed in the vaults of a local bank for safety, until the time of treating it—a nine ton lot being taken to the bank the night previous to the writing of this article—but still a far richer streak has been encountered in a vein lying about 100 feet from this one—the extra rich pay streak is about one foot in width—but it is too rich to last long—one assay running as high as $116,000 to the ton. Besides these extra rich streaks there is a large vein of talc 70 feet in width which is a $20 to $30 grade of milling ore. A mill is being installed by the company at the present time to treat its ores.

Diamondfield Section—Goldfield District

The Diamond=Black Butte Consolidated—four claims in all, consisting of the former properties of the Diamondfield and Black Butte. This property lies northeast of Goldfield about five miles near the town of Diamondfield—north of it.

The Butte shaft is down to the depth of 150 feet; the Quartzite, 200 feet, and the Daisy shaft, 150 feet; besides numerous drifts and cross-cuts.

From the Quartzite shaft, upwards of $200,000 of high grade ore has been taken and shipped, besides a great amount of milling ore on dump, with still a greater amount blocked out The Black Butte Mountain on which these claims lie can be said to be a mountain of a good milling grade of ore entire—besides the high grades.

This property has very recently been acquired by the Schwab-McKane Syndicate and more than probable it will be worked in the extensive manner that is characteristic of these people.

The Jumbo Extension Mining Co. owns six claims and seven fractions in all. The main holdings lie west of the Black Butte and Diamondfield Mining Co. (Diamond-Black Butte Consolidated).

Most of the development work is on what is known as a Gold Coin lease. These leasers have installed a gasoline hoist and are to the depth of 130 feet at the present writing, it being their intention to go down to the 250 foot level before cross-cutting and drifting to any large extent, but some drifting was done on the 50 foot and 100 foot levels—both showing ore of good values. About $8,000 has been shipped from this property with good indications that it will become an extensive shipper of some high grade ore. Assays of $1,700 to $3,000 have been obtained. Three other shafts have been sunk on the same property with good showing.

The company also owns three fractions lying immediately northwest of the Jumbo property.

The Goldfield Diamond Mining Co owns four claims lying south and immediately adjoining the Jumbo Extension and southwest of the Black Butte claims, between these two properties and the town of Diamondfield.

Several shallow shafts and numerous cross-cuts have been made along the main ledge for a distance of 900 feet. This prospect work, showing up the ledge, represents the displacement of 7,000 cubic feet of rock. This ledge is a quartz one showing a good width. There are also three or more other ledges on property—one, the Gold Coin ledge has lately been traced a distance of 2,000 feet on this property.

Values are known to be on all the claims, and on the main ledge, where work is done, assays all run from a few dollars to $1,700. At two different points the high values were encountered.

Shaft No. 4, where it was decided to sink to a depth so as to block out the ore and have stoping ground, was sunk 25 feet north of ledge so as to encounter ledge at about 60 foot depth. At a depth of 55 feet a large flow of water was encountered coming from the ledge. While water is a most valuable asset it has delayed work until a steam hoist and pumping plant, which have been ordered, can be installed.

Shafts No. 1, 2, and 3 are to a depth of 60, 31, and 27 feet respectively on the same ledge.

The directors of the company are considering plans for a stamp mill to be built on the grounds—more than probable it will be a 20-stamp one.

Knickerbocker Mountain Section—Goldfield District

The Dixie Mining Co. owns five claims lying three miles due east of Goldfield. Development work consists of double compartment shaft 300 feet in depth with levels run on the 70 foot, 110 foot and the present work being done on the 300 foot level, besides this there is one tunnel in hill 265 feet, and another one sixty feet above which is in 210 feet. These tunnels are connected with a winze. Both tunnels encountered body of milling ore thirty feet in width, with average value of $25. The workings on 70 and 110 foot levels are all in ore and they also pass through a twenty foot vein on the 300 foot—the ore on these levels averaged over $30. There is a great amount of surface work done.

They are installing a larger engine so as to sink to the water level which they expect to reach in another 200 feet.

BULLFROG DISTRICT

When "Shorty" Harris and Ed Cross made a rich strike seventy-five miles south and east of Goldfield on August 9th, 1904, it brought the third large camp into existence in four years' time. This camp promises not to be out-stripped by any of its predecessors. Within less than six months after ore was first struck on one property in this district the owners were offered, by a very strong company, three millions of dollars for the mine.

Although over 100 miles from the railroad within a year's time seven gasoline hoists have been installed and several others ordered.

There is a bountiful supply of water for domestic and milling purposes. A 20-stamp mill is being constructed and two other companies organized to erect others. Three railroads are building towards the district, the Salt Lake Railroad from Las Vegas, while "Borax" Smith is building from Ludlow, California, on the main line of the Santa Fe, from the south, and the Tonopah railroad intends extending down from Goldfield on the north, work of actual construction to start in a few days.

The mineralized district is an extra large one and can be said to be divided into five sections—that adjacent to the town of Rhyolite and Bullfrog; Original Bullfrog Section, three miles west; Gold Bar Section, four miles northwest; Crystal Springs Section, seven miles north, and the section east of the Amargosa River, seven miles east of Rhyolite.

(*OCTOBER 1st, 1905*)

Beginning at the right hand side and going around the Horseshoe, is first Ladd Mountain, which lies east of the town, Montgomery Mountain, lying northeast, other mountains, unnamed, lying north and Bonanza Mountain, lying west.

Amargosa Gold Mining Co. owns nine claims lying on the Amargosa flat, about 1,500 feet south of Ladd Mountain. They have a well timbered shaft which is to the depth of 328 feet. They intend sinking further after which they will commence to cross-cut going after the veins that traverse Ladd Mountain. They are going to install a gasoline hoist in the very near future.

The Montana=Bullfrog Mining Co., five claims on the southern and western slopes of Ladd Mountain. They have a 200 foot tunnel from the west side besides other development work and have encountered a four foot ledge, assays $100, and large bodies of milling ore. The large vein has not been encountered as yet.

The Bullfrog Mining Co. of Nevada, ten claims covering almost the entire western slope of Ladd Mountain, a greater portion of the eastern slope and part of the southern slope. On the western slope is a well defined vein running northerly and southerly, average width of 150 feet, which carries an excellent grade of milling ore interlaced with streaks, or strata, of talc which carries assay values of $1,000 to $5,000 per ton. A cross-cut tunnel is being driven from the extreme western point and at a point 350 feet from the portal they encountered a vein and have gone into the vein 50 feet. Values have increased. They have also started sinking shaft at present time on vein.

There are five distinct veins between the western point of Ladd Mountain and the eastern.

The Bullfrog National Bank Gold Mining Co. consists of three claims on the southern end of Ladd Mountain. They have installed a 25 h. p. gasoline hoist with all necessary auxiliary machinery. They have sunk a shaft 200 feet in depth with levels at each 100 foot. They are drifting on the 100 foot and cross-cutting on the 200 foot. They have a good grade of milling ore and in another six months expect to have a mill in operation.

Mr. Patrick and associates, chief owners of the above property, are piping water from Beatty Ranch, a distance of several miles. They have a flow of 250,000 gallons every twenty-four hours. This will be used for milling and other purposes as it is needed.

The Yankee Girl, three and a half claims, is owned mainly by the National Bank people and is an extension of that property on the north. They also have a gasoline hoist installed. They have a shaft sunk 200 feet and intend to cross-cut or drift as soon as they go through the present foot-wall of contact they are in.

The Shoshone=National Bank Mining Co. owns a group of fractions, consisting of 66 acres—extending from the National Bank, north-east through the dip on to the Montgomery and Rainbow Mountains. They have a shaft 50 foot deep and 50 foot cross-cut. They have milling ore and stringers of manganese quartz, but main ore bodies have not been encountered yet.

The Four Ace Mining Co.—62 acres—composed mainly of fractions, joins Schwab-McKane's Crystal on the south. They are just starting development work. Have had assays on surface from $4 to $26. Owned by New York people—Stillman F. Kneeland, Advocate General of New York, being president. They have two shifts working and are going after the Montgomery-Shoshone vein. (During the month of October after the writing of this article a good grade of ore was encountered).

The Crystal Mining Co.—three and a fraction claims, lying on the south slope of Montgomery Mountain and southward. Owned by the Schwab-McKane people. They have sunk shaft 100 feet on the west end and are cross-cutting and also have started to sink another shaft on the east and are going after the Montgomery-Shoshone vein.

The Montgomery=Shoshone Mines Co., of Bullfrog consists of a group of claims lying on the ridge between Rhyolite and Beatty, on Montgomery Mountain. It is termed "The Infant Wonder of the Desert." Ore was discovered on this property in January and in less than six months the owners were offered $3,000,000 for the property. Considering the age of the property and the work done it is said by all that have examined it to be a world beater. Assays run from $100 to $15,000. There have been numerous drifts run and it is estimated there are several millions of dollars already blocked out. Besides large ledges of quartz, there is a large body of pink talc which carries values. Several shipments have been made. Numerous improvements have been made among them being office buildings, large bunk house, boarding house, and large ore bins.

The Shoshone=Polaris Mining Co.—two claims lying due west and immediately adjoining the big mine, Montgomery-Shoshone. Development work consists of 100 foot shaft with tunnel, cross-cut of 120 feet on the 50 foot level and drift 90 feet—and at bottom of shaft, drift 75 feet and cross-cut 20 feet. The drift work has all been on four foot vein of quartz averaging $75. All drift work has been on ore—picked assays running very high, but average of ore $76.

The Montgomery Mountain Mining Co.—90 acres lying on the western slope of Montgomery Mountain, adjoining the Polaris and the Montgomery-Shoshone, lying south of the one and southwest of the other. They have tunnelled into the mountain from the west 230 feet and at about 150 feet they encountered a nine foot vein of $30 to $40 ore. They are still driving on so as to catch the Montgomery-Shoshone dyke.

The Providence Mining Co.—three claims and two fractions, lying immediately adjoining and to the northeast of the Montgomery-Shoshone. Development work consists of shaft 100 feet and cross-cutting from there, which they have done to 100 feet—having encountered the vein but have not received returns from the assayer.

The Lucky Jack=Shoshone Mining Co.—one and a fraction claims, lying south of east of the Providence and 600 feet northeast of the Montgomery-Shoshone. Development work consists of shaft 106 feet in depth and contract has been let for 100 foot cross-cut for purpose of encountering ore shoot of the Montgomery-Shoshone vein. As a gasoline hoist has been ordered it will soon be equipped with one. The Montgomery-Shoshone vein enters property 275 feet from the south end line and traverses the property at angle of 60 degrees east of north. Values secured run about the same as values in same kind of rock in the Shoshone but as yet the main ore shoot has not been encountered.

The Bullfrog=Red Oak Co.—one and a fraction claims besides a tunnel site. The property lies 1,500 feet east and north of the main workings of the Montgomery-Shoshone. Development work consists of a 100 foot shaft with 40 foot cross-cut on 50 foot level and they are preparing to cross-cut on the 100 foot level. They have struck some values and are going after the Montgomery-Shoshone ledge which more than probably goes through the property. They have also started tunnelling and ultimately will go 1,500 feet and possibly 3,000 feet. A gasoline hoist has also been ordered for this property.

The Bullfrog=Steinway Mining Co.—two claims lying 600 feet west of the Polaris and 900 feet west of the Montgomery-Shoshone. A gasoline hoist has been installed. Development work consists of shaft 100 feet in depth and drift of 75 feet in four foot vein of quartz ore, which averages $60. They are at the present sinking so as to go down to the 200 foot level.

The Elkhorn Mining Co. owns three claims, two of which lie immediately adjoining the Perry-Montgomery (Montgomery Mountain) and the Polaris, being on the west of these. There is a shaft 60 feet in depth which is being sunk to the 100 foot level at which time they intend to cross-cut to catch the ledge. The third claim is on Bonanza Mountain and adjoins the Great Eastern on the north. Development work on this has not as yet started.

The Gibraltar Mining Syndicate owns upwards of of 170 acres taking in the southwest, south and southeast slopes of Bonanza Mountain. The development work consists of a main tunnel in 231 feet, another tunnel on what is known as Number 4 ledge and two shafts, 62 and 115 feet deep, cross-cutting, etc. Main tunnel has encountered two ledges so far, one of which is two feet wide, the other seven feet—both of which average a good grade of milling ore. Number 2 ledge has been drifted on about 40 feet. The tunnel is being continued so as to encounter ledge Number 3, also ledges Number 4, 5, and 6. The other tunnel, or drift, is on ledge Number 4, which ledge is about 10 feet in width, all of which runs high with ten inches of exceedingly high grade (assays running $15,000 to the ton). Another tunnel has been started on this same ledge but running on a level some 80 feet lower. The 62 foot shaft is on Number 6 ledge and the 115 foot shaft is on Tramp ledge. Values have been encountered in almost all parts of shafts.

The Bullfrog=Eclipse Mining Co.—four claims joining the Gibraltar and the Tramps lying on the north of them, and taking in the crest of Bonanza Mountain. The development work consists of Hobo shaft of 150 feet which is an inclined shaft of about 50 degrees, going down the vein, with drifts at 60 foot level. Vein started on surface four feet in width which was followed until 65 feet was obtained, by which time it had widened out to ten feet and became too large for shaft work; below that depth the shaft was made a six-foot shaft following the hanging wall.

The entire ten feet contained high grade milling, also high grade shipping ore.

The Lester shaft, on the Lester vein, is same incline as the above shaft, and is to a depth of 65 feet. The shaft, six-foot, follows the hanging wall, no cross-cutting having been done as yet to catch the foot-wall; all parts carry good milling values.

The Eclipse shaft on the main Tramp ledge is to a vertical depth of 75 feet, following the vein. Ledge has been drifted on 50 feet north and cross-cut twice from drift, showing fourteen and fifteen feet solid manganese quartz, and they are taking out both shipping and high grade milling ore, the entire amount of ore making a wonderful average in values per ton. A cross-cut is run from Eclipse shaft, 102 feet towards the Hobo vein, so as to encounter the Hobo ledge at depth of 220 feet.

About 200 sacks from the Eclipse shaft and 300 sacks from the Hobo shaft have been sacked with high grade ore for shipping.

The Tiger tunnel is in about 143 feet on the Tiger vein. This vein is a good 12 feet in width. This ledge carries more silver than the other veins—the values being about equally divided between gold and silver.

In all there are four good veins being worked—running parallel with each other—and good indications of more being encountered as cross-cutting is carried on.

The Tramps consists of two full claims lying on Bonanza Mountain to the south of the Eclipse property. It is traversed by five or six veins on which more or less development work has been done. Good values have been encountered.

The Denver Bullfrog Annex Mining Co. owns three fractions on Bonanza Mountain—the Louisville fraction consists of seven acres, lying between the Gibraltar, the Tramps and the Eclipse properties; the Denver fraction, four acres, joins the Denver on the south and the Eclipse on the north; the Lookout fraction, thirteen acres, lies further north being about one quarter of a mile north of the Denver property. Development work consists of tunnel on the Louisville, which is in about 130 feet, the entire distance following the hanging wall of a twelve foot vein. Two winzes have been started in tunnel, one in about 90 feet, the other 110 feet. The first winze is sunk on ore shoot; assays showing from $40 to $308 ore. A fifty foot incline shaft following vein is sunk on north part of fraction and vein is drifted on about 20 feet at bottom of shaft. This vein is what is known as Number 4 vein of the Gibraltar where a big strike has occurred. It shows values all the way down.

No development work has been done as yet on other two fractions.

The Bullfrog Golden Scepter Mining Co.—owns fifteen claims in all, some of which are fractions. They lie on the eastern slope of Bonanza Mountain extending from the Gibraltar, on the south, and adjoining the Great Eastern, lying south and east of that property. It also extends east taking in part of the town site of Rhyolite. Development work which has very recently been started, consists of 50 foot shaft, two cross-cuts at bottom of shaft to the vein known as the Hobo vein, and a tunnel 50 foot in, located at the base of the mountain, which will cut the mountain at about 450 feet below apex. With this tunnel they expect to cross-cut Louisville, Hobo, Tramps, and Eclipse vein.

There is also a shaft being sunk on the north side fraction, on the Tramp vein and a tunnel being run on the same vein at the north end by the Murphy-Vorhees leasees. This vein as open is four or five feet wide. A good milling grade of ore was encountered in shaft and also good values secured in the north side fraction tunnel,— the least assay in this being $17.20.

The Great Eastern Mining Co. owns three claims lying on the eastern slope of Bonanza Mountain. A gasoline hoist has been installed. They are below the 150 foot level and are going to the 200 foot level before they again drift. Some drifting was done on the 50 foot and also 100 foot level and on the 150 foot level 150 feet of drifting was done and 50 feet of cross-cutting. The ledge matter exposed consists of a free milling grade of ore. Some very high assays have been obtained. The writer takes occasion to say that the development work that is being carried on is being done in an A 1 workmanship manner.

The Denver Mining Co. owns two claims, lying on Bonanza Mountain, west of the Eclipse group and immediately adjoining it. Three tunnels have been made. Tunnel Number 1, or the one near the top, drifts in the vein, 125 feet, tunnel Number 2, lying on the same vein 50 feet lower, 250 feet in, and tunnel Number 3 lies 75 feet below Number 2 and drifts 275 feet. They have stoped from Number 2 a distance of 25 feet and 100 feet in length and have sunk winze in Number 2 about 20 feet.

About forty tons of ore is sacked ready for shipment. It is expected to net an average of $200 per ton. Assays have been secured that have run as high as $10,000.

The Frazier et al Property—a property consisting of seventy-six acres lying along the apex of Bonanza Mountain joining and lying to the north of the Great Eastern. It is being developed by F. O. Frazier of Rhyolite who has associated with him some Los Angeles parties. There is a working tunnel of 75 feet and it is expected that a body of ore will be encountered at 150 feet. The Denver vein is expected to be struck at that distance.

The Bullfrog=Venture=Nevada Gold Mining Co. owns eight claims, lying a short distance from the Peerless and Denver and the ledges are the continuation of ledges of those claims. There are three veins on property which have been drifted and sunk on. Values show a milling grade with good prospects for greater values.

The Rhyolite Rose Gold Mining Co. owns seven claims lying in two groups. One group of five claims being about three quarters of a mile north of Rhyolite on the northern slope of Bonanza Mountain, while the other two claims are located on Red Mountain, two miles north of Rhyolite. Both groups are traversed with strong ledges. On the group of five claims quite a bit of development work has been done with very encouraging results. A shaft 50 feet deep has been sunk and many cross-cuts and drifts run. Large bodies of low grade milling ore have been encountered and a rich streak of manganese quartz cut, which assays up in the hundreds.

The Bullfrog Chief Mining Co. owns five claims lying northwest of the Great Eastern property at about 100 rods distance. They have had fair values on the surface and have started development work. Two shafts are being sunk—one on the Chief claim and the other on the Good Will claim.

The Original Bullfrog Section—Bullfrog District

The Original Bullfrog Mining Co. owns two full claims, lying three miles due west of Rhyolite. It has an ore peculiar to itself. It is purely a quartz ledge, some places thirty feet in width, all of which carries values of a milling grade and exceedingly high grade ore has been obtained in some parts of ledge. The ore carrying the large values is of a very green hue, being a bullfrog green, and as this is the original discovery and the mining district received its name—Bullfrog—on account of this highly colored ore, it consequently has become very popular with the residents of the district for jewelry. The stone, which is freely sprinkled with gold, takes a very nice polish and is made into cuff buttons, scarf pins, etc.

Development work in the mine consists of a main tunnel 400 feet in length and two shafts, one 64 feet in depth and the other 144 feet. Three shipments have been made from this property, in some of which the ore ran over $900 to the ton. A 20 h. p. gasoline hoist is being installed at the present time.

The Big Bullfrog Mining Co. owns one and a fraction claims, lying one half mile south and west of the Original Bullfrog. They also have installed a gasoline hoist, with all necessary auxiliary machinery. The development work consists of shaft 115 feet deep with drifts at the 100 foot level. It is the management's intention to continue sinking to the 200 foot level before again drifting. The vein is a well defined one.

The Bullfrog Extension consists of four full claims —three of which lie east and south and immediately adjoining the Original Bullfrog, and the fourth claim on the north side of the Original Bullfrog. The Original Bullfrog ledge continues through at least half the property. Development work consists of shaft fifty-five feet deep with cross-cuts at bottom which show up the ledge, also an incline tunnel 180 feet in length which cross-cuts the ledge, which is about fifty feet in width. Good values have been secured on this property.

The Original Bullfrog Extension consists of two full claims, lying north of the Original Bullfrog property and is a continuation of the same ledge. Development work consists of a double compartment shaft, 122 feet in depth, and they are continuing down so as to encounter ledge which they expect to encounter in another 40 feet.

The Goldfrog Mining Co. owns two full claims, situated one half mile due north of the Original Bullfrog. Development work consists of tunnel 125 feet and shows up good looking rock, also a seven foot vein of talc. At the time of the writer's visit to this property the management was out and the exact values encountered were not obtainable.

Gold Bar Section—Bullfrog District

The Gold Bar, five full claims and two fractions; two miles north and west of the Original Bullfrog and four miles northwest of Rhyolite. 800 feet of development work has been done on this property and every foot of it is in ore. On the surface a mineralized zone can be seen traversing the property for upwards of 2,000 feet and of the width of 200 feet. This zone all pans and carries a value on the surface of $18 and $20.

Development work consists of Number 1 shaft 150 feet in depth with 50 foot cross-cut on 50 foot level, in ore (assays of which run $89). Neither wall was touched. On the 150 foot level, they have drifted 100 feet each way and have cross-cut the vein 68 feet from the hanging wall towards the foot wall, which has not been found yet. Number 2 shaft is 50 feet deep with 65 foot cross-cut and neither wall found. The above workings have all been in a good grade of milling ore; while Number 3 shaft, which is 50 feet in depth, is sunk on rich ore shoot.

(During the month of October and after this article was written, a body of ore running very high was encountered in addition to this large body of lower grade ore).

The Bullfrog=Homestake Mine consists of three claims. It immediately adjoins the Gold Bar and that same ledge continues on this property for a distance of 1,500 feet. Values run $40 to $50.

The Bullfrog=Gold Bar Western consists of four and a fraction claims, situated on Rheinhart Mountain, joins the Gold Bar and side-lines the Homestake. Development work will start on the property in a very few days.

Crystal Springs Section—Bullfrog District

In the Crystal Springs section of the Bullfrog District there are numerous properties but very little development work has as yet been done.

The Mayflower=Bullfrog Mining Co.—four claims is worthy of exceptional mention. It has a well defined ledge from thirty to forty feet in width, which all pans, with streak of quartz six feet in width which runs $25 to $40—talc on the wall runs still higher. The ledge has been cross-cut, also some drifting on vein has been done and shaft sunk to a depth of thirty-five feet. Quite an amount of stock has been sold and development work on a larger scale will soon commence. This property lies one and a half miles west of Crystal Springs.

East of Amargosa River—Bullfrog District

The Bullfrog Royal Mining Co. owns two claims, lying one-half mile east of the Amargosa River. A strong ledge six feet in width extends the entire distance of the two claims, 3,000 feet, the claims end-lining each other. Development work consists mainly in prospecting main ledge. Assays from company's workings run from $16 to $180, gold and silver, with an average of $42, while leasers have recently struck a rich pay streak from six inches to twelve inches which runs exceedingly high—the least assay running above $200. Development work will soon be carried on on this property extensively. As it lies 1,000 feet above the river and facing it, the property is a good tunnelling proposition.

The Kismet Gold Mining Co. owns five claims lying east of the Amargosa River. It has an immense quartzite dyke vein on which two incline shafts have been sunk; one 56 feet deep and the other 66 feet, with drift connecting the two. Some high assays have been secured.

Among other properties which are worthy of mention, lying in this section, can be named the **Lige Harris,** on which some high assays have been secured; the **Wild Cat,** which is a copper, gold and silver property; the **Blue Jay,** assays from which have shown good values; **Kawich=Bullfrog,** consisting of twenty-eight claims divided into six groups, good assays secured and shaft sunk on the Greenback group; the **Sunset,** on which shaft has been sunk and cross-cutting done, assays running as high as $32.50, and the **Diamond=Queen** group, five claims, which has a large, 300 foot in width ledge —being a flourine ore, assays averaging from $18 to $40 in gold.

The Lind Mines Co., of Bullfrog, owns nine full claims in the Bullfrog District, lying in the Funeral Range, southwest of Rhyolite and near the California-Nevada state line. There are four large ledges of milling ore on the claims, besides float which assays high, has been found on claims, but this large pay shoot has not been found as yet.

ECHO CANYON

Several good properties have been found in Echo Canyon. This Canyon lies off of Death Valley near the Furnace Creek Ranch and is only about thirty-five or forty miles, by a bee-line, almost due south, from Rhyolite and Bullfrog.

The Hicks=Leavitt property in this Canyon consists of several claims. The main ledge, which is fourteen feet wide, is composed of a free milling, white sugar quartz. A shaft has been sunk 51 feet and assays average about $50. It has recently been bonded for $150,000.

The Paymal-Bradshaw property consists of about twenty claims divided into three groups. The main ledge is about twelve feet in width. Assays run as high as $60 and very little work done.

The Gold Rock, six claims, with assays as high as $64.20 and the **Gold Mint,** five claims, from which an assay as high as $35.15 was secured, are two other new properties in this canyon. Very little work done.

THE OLDER DISTRICTS

(SEPTEMBER 1st, 1905.)

In giving a synopsis of the new gold fields in Southern Nevada, it would not be right to altogether pass up the older camps in that part of the state, as they seem to be more or less in the same mineralized zone that passes through the Comstock on the north—southeastwardly through Goldfield and the Bullfrog Districts to the Searchlight and El Dorado Canyon Districts on the south. Among the more prominent of these older districts can be mentioned the Johnnie, (formerly known as the Montgomery), Sandy, Good Springs, Crescent, Searchlight, and El Dorado Canyon.

It was the pleasure of the writer to take in all of these camps with the one exception of the latter, the El Dorado Canyon District, which he very much regrets he was unable to visit. They all have a good showing and with better transportation facilities, which the greater share of them are getting, which means better and cheaper living, together with improved mining machinery for the treatment of ore, and new strikes being made in several of these districts—it means wonders to the southern part of the state, which has been and is already, without these additional advantages, a big producer.

THE JOHNNIE DISTRICT

(54 miles south and east of Bullfrog District)

The Johnnie Mine is owned by the Johnnie Consolidated Gold Mining Co. and is situated three miles north of the town of Johnnie. It is an old property, it being the pioneer of this section—twelve years old. It is being worked at present on the 600 foot level. There is one mile of underground workings; 30,000 tons of ore blocked out. Ore averages $12 to $15 per ton. The ore bodies run from six to fifteen feet in width and values getting better as they go down. The 500 foot level averaged $20 and the 600 foot will more than probably go better. 8,000 tons of ore milled from the mine above the 300 foot level gave average of $18 per ton, yielding $14 per ton in gold bullion, balance tailings.

The formation is a large quartzite ledge overlaid by shales and massive limestone.

The owners have piped water from the Grapevine Springs, two miles distant, for camp and milling purposes. They have their own boarding house and bunk houses, and have selected a site for a modern stamp mill and cyanide plant, which they expect to install soon. There are from fifteen to twenty men working and when mill is completed the force will be greatly increased.

The Bullfrog-Johnnie is located 3,500 feet south of the Johnnie Consolidated Gold Mining Co.'s property. It is located on east and west lead, while the Johnnie is a north and south lead. Values here run as high as $40 per ton and the ledge averages two to six feet in width. The property consists of five claims—100 acres.

Lucelle and Mae Mines—owned by G. F. Moser, superintendent of the Johnnie mines—joins the Bullfrog-Johnnie on the south. Values and conditions are also similar to that property.

The Chispa Mines—located about one mile southwest of town of Johnnie, is a property of nearly as much note as the Johnnie mine, having been operated for years. It reached a depth of 350 feet and produced about $50,000 in gold bullion.

The burning of a 10-stamp mill was the cause of prior shut-down of this property, but it is stated operation will again be resumed in October of this year.

The Johnnie District will experience a decided revival this Fall no doubt, and a number of what are now prospects will prove remunerative mines the next year or two. The "Borax" Smith Railroad will come within twelve miles of this district.

Mineral Flat is a territory lying just west of the Johnnie mines on the edge of Ash Meadows where numerous big ledges and good values have lately been found. Mineral Flat will, no doubt, produce something of note next year.

SANDY

The Nevada Keystone Mine is an old property that has been a big bullion producer. It was formerly known as the Keystone Mine and is situated seven miles northeast of Sandy. Its general run of ore averaged about $30 but masses of it will go many thousands. They have a Huntington mill and cyanide plant located at Sandy and were cyaniding tailings when writer visited it. They are at a depth of 900 feet. They usually employ about forty men. Elevation, 2,700 feet.

The Green Monster is considered a good lead property. It is situated north and east of Sandy and west of Good Springs. It is owned by the Hearst estate and has been worked to the depth of 400 feet. It is carbonate and galena with contacts of light and dark lime. It has lead, copper and also good silver values.

GOOD SPRINGS

The town of Good Springs is nicely nestled in a large valley surrounded by mountains containing many good mining properties and prospects. It is situated seven and a half miles from the new Salt Lake Road, and it expects to reap some advantage from the advent of its close proximity.

An abundance of water can be procured at a very few feet and it is a very neat little village for an out-of-the-way place, which it has been heretofore.

The Chiquite consists of twelve claims, lying eight miles east of Good Springs, and is considered one of the leading mines of the district. It is a gold property and has had assays run as high as $21,000 to the ton. They are only to a depth of 150 feet but the present average of ore runs $100. It has a lime and porphyry contact.

Red Cloud is a gold property—depth, 200 feet. There has just been installed on this property a new gasoline hoist and cyanide plant and is the best equipped mine in the district. The ore averages $25 and there have been assays run as high as $500 on this property.

Boss Mine is a gold and copper property. It has been sunk to a depth of 175 feet; has a ten to twelve foot ledge, averages $15 gold and 18% copper—lime contact. This property is not working now but will resume soon.

Columbia is a copper property of high grade. It is situated about four and a half miles from Good Springs. High values.

May Kirby is west of Good Springs four miles. Lead and silver property and the values run good. It belongs to an estate and is not being operated at present. It is thought the estate will be adjusted within a year when it will again resume operations. **Iron Gold** is a gold property belonging to the same estate.

CRESCENT DISTRICT

The Crescent Mining District is an old district lying near the Nevada-California state line, and about 175 miles south and east from Bullfrog District, near the new town of Nippeno, California, on the New Salt Lake Railroad.

As it has cost so much for freighting and treating gold heretofore, and as the ore did not as a rule run high in the district, consequently it has not developed as the richer districts of its age have in the state, but the finding of some rich ore, in May of this year, on what is known as the Lucky Dutchman property, has again caused eyes to look in this direction.

The Nippeno Mine is located two and a half miles east of the town of Crescent. It is a property that has been worked with a small force for some years and can be said to be the only mine of any prominence in the district, on which much work has been done. There has been more work done on this mine than all the rest put together. Up to date it has been mainly development work of which they have done 1,700 feet and have 10,000 ton of ore in sight, with an average of $17.50 per ton.

The vein is a northwest and southeast one, being a contact vein with hanging wall of granite and foot-wall of diorite. At the present time the owners have a force at work developing for water, after which they intend to put in a modern stamp mill and cyanide plant. It is owned by a close corporation and is considered one of the coming properties of the southern part of the state.

Among the other older and newer properties and prospects in the districts are the following:—

The Tiger, on the north of Crescent, has shipped ore that averaged about $40. It is a gold and silver property and $40 gold and 208 oz. of silver assay has been procured.

but average of ore runs from $12 to $20. It has a massive quartz ledge and its shaft is 125 feet in depth.

Legal Tender, four miles east of Crescent, has shipped ore. Has vein from five to seven feet in width.

Red Star — twenty-two foot vein of ore. Gold averages $9.40 per ton.

Double Standard—silver and gold property, belonging to Dan Sullivan and others of Denver, Colorado.

Col. Sellers is a copper and gold property, joining the Lucky Dutchman, from which a great amount of ore has been shipped.

Sheerer Mine joins the town site on the south. It consists of six claims. A shaft of forty feet has been sunk and some drifting done. Fair values received.

White Rock has been sunk upon, 55 feet. The vein is a true fissure one. Assays have run as high as $200 but ore averages $12.

The Calivada is considered one of the best gold properties in this section. It consists of five claims— three in Nevada two in California, hence the name— Calivada.

Turquoise Property

A few years ago in this district about three miles east of Crossman's Springs, a noted watering place known by all the pioneers and emigrants going through the desert, George Simmons, an old timer, ran across what has since been more than probably the most noted turquoise mine in the world. It was some time before he was able to get capital interested in it but finally he got Charles F. Woods & Co., of New York, large dealers of gems and precious stones—interested. Since then the property has been worked as needed and many a gem has been taken out that has brought $1,000 and it is said that the aggregate sales would run into many millions from this mine and it is practically untouched. These gems have been found in a dyke of great width and about one mile in length. This company owns upwards of thirty claims altogether in this region and practically has a corner on the turquoise market.

One of the notable features of this turquoise mine is the fact that it was worked in ancient times—by whom it is hard to tell—possibly by the Aztecs, possibly by others—but that it was worked is manifested by several signs. There have been many hammers hewn out of stone, stone slabs and other rude tools used to mine and polish the gems found embedded in the earth. As pieces of charcoal have also been found it looks as though they used a fire in some process of their mining. The hammers are very plentiful, have been uncovered in great numbers and are to-day to be run across quite frequently. Some of them are in the earth some depth—the rock has either disintregated and soil formed and covered them up or else they were covered up by these ancient miners when they had to abandon the mines. Some of the largest trees of this part of the state have since grown from this soil that overlays these rude implements of mining.

SEARCHLIGHT DISTRICT

The principal town in the Searchlight District is Searchlight. It lies in Nevada twenty-two miles east of Nippeno, California, on the Salt Lake route, and thirty miles north of Manvel, California, on the Santa Fe. The district is about seven years old and is becoming better with age. But little is heard of this district in the outside world but they are continually blocking out the ore and getting out the bullion. There are 60 stamps working continuously night and day and more stamp mills are being erected.

One of the largest mines—The Quartette—in the country is located here. One of the notable features of the camp is that practically each of the mines is owned by two or three people and the most of them are not stocked, if stocked more than probable the corporation is a close one and no stock for sale.

The Quartette—consisting of nine claims. They have two 20-stamp mills, one, which is running continuously, located at the mine, while they also have another one located at the river, sixteen miles east. The mine is down to the 900 foot depth and over two miles of underground development work has been done. This is the largest mine in the district and is noted as being the third largest in importance in the country. With the present capacity there is enough ore in sight to run seven years. The average of the ore that is saved runs $22.

The Duplex—consists of seven claims located on what is known as Searchlight Hill. It is equipped with a 10-stamp mill. It is to a depth of 432 feet with 4,000 feet of underground work. The ore averages a good $12 all the way through. The water is being pumped out of the mine preparatory to sinking to lower level. G. F. Colton and A. L. Glassell are the sole owners.

The Cyrus Noble Mining Co. is a close corporation owning five or six patented claims. They have a 15 h. p. gasoline hoist and a cyanide plant, but have heretofore leased a mill, but are constructing a 10-stamp mill of their own this Fall. Most of their work has been confined to blocking out ore and they have only milled about 1,200 tons, which averaged a little over $30 per ton. They are to a level of 476 feet. The property is a gold and silver proposition—it running more silver than any other property in the camp. It runs eighteen oz. of silver to one oz. of gold.

Good Hope consists of three claims just north of the Quartette. It is owned by Fred Colton. They have shipped ore and got good returns. There is 1,500 feet of development work done on this property.

The Searchlight Parallel Gold Mining Co. has five claims just north of Cyrus Noble mine—same lead. They have shipped some ore and have milled some. The grade of ore is very similar to the Cyrus Noble, running a great deal in silver. They have sunk to the 200 foot depth and have had extra good showing in shaft; have also drifted some. It is the only chloriding property in the camp.

The Santa Fe is six claims, joining the above property to the east. It is said they produced $60,000 in a three months mill test. They have sunk to 170 foot depth from which point they are drifting.

The Southern Nevada Mining and Milling Co. joins the Santa Fe on the north—lying about one and one half miles north of town. They have a 10-stamp mill and a 100 ton cyanide plant. They have produced $316,000 and at the time of the writing of this article they were in process of cyaniding which will bring it up to $350,000. They are 300 feet deep and have done 3,000 feet of development work.

The Searchlight Mining and Milling Co. has six claims and joins the above property on the north. They are erecting at present a 10-stamp mill that will be started this month. They have sunk a 350 foot shaft and have large bodies of ore exposed. Recent mill tests for three months are said to have produced $90,000. This property has a very good outlook.

The Pompeii Mining Co. consists of seven claims, adjoins the Searchlight on the north. They are the farthest north of any property in the proven mining belt. They have sunk a shaft to the depth of 260 feet with levels run exposing the ore bodies. They are also equipping mines with machinery preparatory to sinking deeper. They have made mill tests of ore—it running $26.

The New Erie Mining Co. lies four miles east. They have a 10-stamp mill, have sunk shaft 300 feet with levels run. Have made good showing.

Many Prospects

There are many prospects at least thirty good ones in this district, many having appearances of making mines.

EL DORADO CANYON

El Dorado Canyon is a very old camp which has been worked since 1860. It lies eighteen miles north of Searchlight. Many millions of dollars have been taken out of this camp. It has had several years of rest but it again expects to put itself on its old time basis and be one of the world's big producers again.

The Techatticup. Two and a half millions of dollars are said to have come out of this property. The name is an Indian one meaning—White Flower. After being idle for a good number of years it has again resumed operations. They have put up hoist and are sinking shaft so as to develop below old workings.

The old **Wall Street** has produced a great amount of money. This property is owned by Joseph Horton of Philadelphia, same owner as the Techatticup.

The Buster Mine, owned by the Black Hawk Mining Co., has been a large producer heretofore and has resumed operation of late. They have put in new gasoline hoist, have developed water and are putting in dry crushing and cyanide plant. It lies adjoining the Techatticup and is a continuation of the same.

The Black Hawk, extension of the Wall Street, is another good property. Large surface finds said to run as high as $1,000 have been found on this property recently.

BEATTY BULLFROG MINER

$3 Per Year
T. G. NICKLIN, Proprietor

Pioneer Newspaper of Bullfrog District. Honest Mining News. No Fake

BEATTY, NEVADA

THE RHYOLITE HERALD

The Leading Newspaper of the Bullfrog District

$5 PER YEAR

Published at Rhyolite, the Metropolis of the District

CLEMEM & KEENE, Publishers

BULLFROG MINER

BULLFROG, NEVADA

PIONEER PAPER OF BULLFROG

The Greatest Gold Camp the World has ever Seen

$5.00 PER YEAR

SUBSCRIBE FOR

THE GOLDFIELD REVIEW

For Mining News of the Greatest Gold Camp on Earth

$4.00 PER YEAR

T. D. VAN DEVORT, Editor, COLUMBIA, NEVADA

MAIN OFFICE: GOLDFIELD
Esmeralda Hotel

MAIN OFFICE: RHYOLITE
Wells Fargo Office

The Overland Stage Line

Daily Service from GOLDFIELD to RHYO-LITE, BULLFROG and BEATTY, also LAS VEGAS. Leaves Goldfield and Rhyolite every morning at six o'clock. Montana Station at noon. Only 12 hours between Goldfield and Bullfrog District.

4-Horse Coaches
4 Relays En Route

Easy Riding, Thoroughly Braced, Concord Stages

First-Class Horses. Pick of the Desert Best that Can be Procured

FARE, $18.00

50 Lbs. Baggage Free
Express, 5c per Lb.

Carries U. S. Mail and
Wells Fargo Express

B. RAMSEY, Manager

TONOPAH AND GOLDFIELD R. R.
Fast Limited Express Trains
THROUGH SERVICE

To and From the Bonanza Gold Fields of Southern Nevada

(JANUARY 1, 1906, MOUNTAIN TIME)

Lv. San Francisco............ 7:00 P. M.	Lv. Goldfield................... 6:55 A. M.
" Sacramento...............11:15 "	Ar. Tonopah .... 8:05 "
" Reno...................... 8:00 A. M.	Lv. Tonopah .... 8:25 "
Av. Tonopah .... 8:50 P. M.	Ar. Reno .... 7:15 P. M.
Lv. Tonopah .... 9:10 "	" Sacramento............... 3:25 A. M.
Ar. Goldfield ....10:15 "	" San Francisco............ 7:08 "

Pullman Sleepers and Diners between San Francisco, Oakland, Sacramento, Reno, to Tonopah and Goldfield.

TONOPAH AND GOLDFIELD R. R. CO.
JOHN W. BROCK, Pres.　　ALONZO TRIPP, Gen. Pass. Agt.

LAS VEGAS-BULLFROG STAGE

Leaves Las Vegas (on Salt Lake R. R.) and Bullfrog every morning at 6 o'clock. Makes through trip in 34 hours with 5 hours' lay over

7 Changes of Horses. Good Meals En Route
FARE, $25

L. P. KIMBALL, General Manager
LAS VEGAS, NEVADA

FIRST-CLASS STAGE
... FROM ...
Jean, Nev. (on Salt Lake R. R.) to Manse, Nev.

LEAVES TUESDAYS, THURSDAYS AND SATURDAYS
VIA GOODSPRINGS AND SANDY
THE MOST DIRECT ROUTE FOR

Resting Springs, Johnnie and Death Valley Mining Districts

FIRST-CLASS SERVICE.　GOOD RIGS.　CARRIES U. S. MAIL

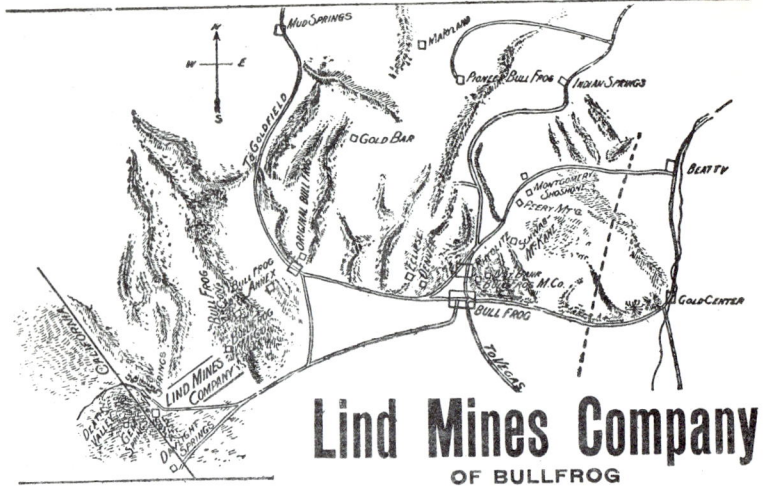

Lind Mines Company
OF BULLFROG

CAPITAL STOCK, $1,000,000; 1,000,000 SHARES PAR VALUE, $1.00 EACH. FULLY PAID, NON-ASSESSABLE. 400,000 SHARES IN TREASURY

Owns a clear title to nine full claims — 180 acres — located southwest of Bullfrog, in Funeral Range, one-half mile east of Nevada-California state line.

Four large ledges of milling ore, running from $4 to $14 outcrop on this property (estimated that hundreds of thousands of tons of ore is in place), also some high grade float has been found running upwards of $500 per ton.

It is for the purpose of developing the large deposits, also to seek this high grade ore that the company offers **a limited amount of treasury stock at 20 cents per share.** Price subject to change without notice.

DIRECTORS AND OFFICERS: JOHN S. COOK, President; H. B. LIND, Vice-President; W. H. GELSTHORPE, Secretary; LOUIS W. BOND; J. H. LANDRETH; JOHN S. COOK, Treasurer

Investigate into the Management; then, if Satisfied, Invest
COMMISSION ALLOWED BROKERS

ADDRESS, LIND MINES CO., OF BULLFROG
DRAWER A. GOLDFIELD, NEVADA

Tonopah-Goldfield Trust Co.

GOLD CENTER, NEVADA

THIS corporation was formerly located at Goldfield, Nevada. Owing to its extensive holdings in the Bullfrog District it removed to Gold Center on December 1, 1905, and is now located there in its new stone building at the corner of Main and Seventh Streets. In addition to its general business of banking and trust functions it has the general management of the Bullfrog-Royal Mining Company, the Decillion Gold Mines Limited, the Wabash-Bull Frog Mines Company and the Bullfrog Belle Mining Company. It is heavily interested in all of these companies and is also the largest owner of the Gold Center Town Site and Water Rights, the latter being the most valuable water-right in the Bullfrog District. In addition to these interests it owns more than twenty of the most valuable mining claims in that district, and is one of the heaviest owners of the Goldfield-Diamond Mining Company in the Goldfield District, the aggregate investments of the Trust Company being more than half a million of dollars.

The town of Gold Center will be the terminal of the railroads from both north and south and the distributing point for all points of the Bullfrog District. It will also be the mill and smelter town of the district. This is insured by the fact that all roads and canyons lead by a down-grade route directly into Gold Center. The Gold Center Ice and Brewing Co. is the largest in Southern Nevada, and a twenty-stamp mill and cyanide plant is now building.

Expert reports and information regarding any properties or enterprises in the Bullfrog District will be furnished by the Trust Company and correspondence is solicited.

THE DIRECTORS AND OFFICERS ARE:
F. Y. WILLIAMS, President; W. D. LAWTON, Vice President;
HON. G. D. MEIKLEJOHN, BEN SCHLOSS, W. M. STANSBURY;
TOM J. GARDNER, Secretary and Cashier

TONOPAH-GOLDFIELD TRUST CO.
GOLD CENTER, NEVADA

FOR SAFETY
LARGE PROFITS
QUICK RETURNS

INVEST in the properties of the BULL FROG MINING DISTRICT, the greatest GOLD CAMP in the world. Get reliable information from us. We have been on the ground since the birth of the camp and know the good and legitimate from the "wild cat."

Address,

BULLFROG INVESTMENT CO.
RHYOLITE, NEV.

Box 1

GOLDFIELD JACK POT MINING & MILLING CO.

Owning seven full claims or 140 acres in the heart of the famous Montezuma District, seven miles west of Goldfield, offer a small block of treasury stock at **Five Cents per Share.** The Montezuma mine which has been paying big profits for 35 years, and which lies one-half mile west of our property, is building a new stamp mill, which will be very accessible for the milling of our ores. Get in on the **ground floor** as we will not sell very much more stock at five cents, as it is bound to advance in value with all the other properties in that section.

Send your applications accompanied with draft, express or money order to the fiscal agent of the company.

MILTON M. DETCH
GOLDFIELD, NEVADA

BOX 1